Praise for *I Choose Victory*

"I feel like I was just mentored while I read *I Choose Victory*. The cadence of this book was a perfect blend of story examples and scriptural references, masterfully woven together with points that will have you making different choices in the battle of identity and perspective. Cynthia navigates the reader through a very vulnerable heart process. She models her own journey in it so you feel safe to ask yourself the hard questions and be authentic as you have some very real people to compare your process to. I highly recommend this as a study book, for book clubs, or as a discipleship or mentoring guide for groups, individuals, and anyone who wants to walk with the victory that you can thrive in on this side of eternity."

Shawn Bolz

Host of *Translating God* on TBN,
Exploring the Industry on CBN, and
Exploring the Prophetic on Charisma Podcast Network
Author of *Translating God, God Secrets, Through the Eyes of Love,* and more

"I love this book, but even more than that, I love Cynthia. She is my friend. She is real and raw and knows what it means to choose victory when there would be so many reasons to sit down in victimhood. Let's lean in and listen."

Sheila Walsh

Author of *Praying Women*

"I have known and admired Cynthia for many years. Her voice is like no other in the media landscape for a reason: her life is like no other. When she writes about overcoming circumstances and moving from victim to victor, she not only talks the talk. She's walked the walk. All of us face adverse and traumatic events in our life—and some much more profound than others. As Cynthia's life story reveals, there is no circumstance we can't get through with God on our side. This is a book worth reading."

Lee Habeeb

Vice President of Content for Salem Radio Network
Host of *Our American Stories* and *Newsweek* columnist

"In *I Choose Victory*, Cynthia shares how she chose to believe the truth of God's Word and the resulting liberty she has found in Christ. Every day, in myriad ways, we are choosing to believe who God says we are or to believe our feelings or someone else's perception. It is time to choose! Choose to believe God. Choose to take Him at His Word and live as a victor instead of a victim. I have been enriched by Cynthia's friendship and testimony. Cynthia has been there. She will be your guide into the life that Christ died to make available to all who will believe and choose!"

Donna Gaines
Founder and president
Arise2Read

"Cynthia Garrett is, to put it mildly, a force of nature. But she is a force of nature in the best possible way, because when you are with her you are forced to see the world through her eyes, and those eyes have seen a lot. What she writes about in *I Choose Victory* isn't nice platitudes and plucky optimism, but is instead born out of a lifetime of overcoming racism, sexism, abuse, and harassment. This is a book written by someone who has every right to play the "victim card," but who has chosen instead to fight back by refusing that label. This isn't a book about one woman who is stronger than everyone else; it is a roadmap for everyone to stand up for themselves by not letting the actions or opinions of others define who you are."

Darren Wilson
Founder and CEO of WP Films

"To know Cynthia Garrett is to be gifted with a breath of fresh air for the soul. As you listen to her share the amazing stories of her life, you know she makes the decision to choose victory every day. She writes as though the reader is a dear friend, sharing heart to heart about past trauma and the beauty of moving forward into emotional healing. You may begin with tears but you will end with joy, courage, and a fresh look at Scripture. This book is an 'every woman' read."

Diane Strack
Founder
She Loves Out Loud

I CHOOSE VICTORY

Cynthia Garrett

I Choose
VICTORY

MOVING FROM VICTIM TO VICTOR

SALEM
BOOKS
an imprint of Regnery Publishing

Salem Books™ is a trademark of Salem Communications Holding Corporation

Regnery® is a registered trademark of Salem Communications Holding Corporation

ISBN: 978-1-68451-051-1
eISBN: 978-1-68451-069-6

Library of Congress Control Number: 2019956083

Published in the United States by
Salem Books
An imprint of Regnery Publishing
A Division of Salem Media Group
300 New Jersey Ave NW
Washington, DC 20001
www.Regnery.com

Manufactured in the United States of America

10 9 8 7 6 5 4 3 2 1

Books are available in quantity for promotional or premium use. For information on discounts and terms, please visit our website: www.Regnery.com.

Contents

Preface

This book is about victory. It's about staring in the face of the things that have tried, sometimes repeatedly, to make you a victim and finally finding your voice and yelling, "Enough is enough! I will not be silenced into fading away any longer. I will live. I will speak. I will take care of me." The simple reality is that, while people around the world experience harsh realities and abuse daily, victory is born of a refusal to reside in pain.

One of the wisest sisters I have is Sheila Walsh, cohost of the TV Show Life Today with James and Betty Robison *and a bestselling author of more than five million books. Her vulnerability is balanced with an inner strength. When I met her, I knew right away she had a tremendous story to tell about choosing victory for her life. I asked her about a time she felt she lived with a victim's mindset and how she overcame it; this is what she had to say.*

—Cynthia Garrett

Sheila Walsh: My father was a very loving, strong, godly man. But when I was very young, he suffered from a brain aneurysm—and after that, his personality changed, and he turned his rage on me.

I vividly remember the last time I saw my father. I was about six years old, and I turned just in time to realize he was about to bring his cane down on my skull. I don't remember whether

I pulled his cane from him or I pushed it, but he lost his balance and hit the ground hard in our living room. He just lay there, making awful noises. The last look I saw in his eyes was one of absolute hatred, which was hard for me to process as a child.

That day, my father was taken off to what was called, in those days, our local lunatic asylum. He managed to escape one night, and they found him the following morning. He had drowned himself in the river that runs through our town.

Even though I was a child, I felt as if I had brought the house down on my family. My mom lost her husband; my sister and my brother lost their father. We had to move out of the town where we lived and into a small home—government housing.

The question I asked all my growing up years was, "What did my father see in me that made him hate me so much?" I wasn't able to process that he had a serious brain injury that impacted his personality. So I lived with this feeling of "there's just something wrong with me." I see it so often with the women I have the privilege of speaking with and ministering to—that they see themselves as victims of circumstances and believe nothing is going to change.

Cynthia Garrett: *It would have been perfectly understandable for you to accept the victim's narrative of your life. Why did you choose victory over a victim's mindset?*

SW: God began delivering me from that mindset when I was a co-host of *The 700 Club*. Eventually, all the stuff that I just shoved into the cellar of my soul began to take its toll. It was almost as if I was living on the edge of a volcano and the rumble was just getting louder every day. And so I fell apart one morning on national television. I think by that evening or certainly the end of that week, I was in a psychiatric hospital myself. I remember feeling as if my life was really over. But I had an interesting experience.

Sometimes, when you're in a really bad place, nighttime is really dark. That's the hardest time. And that's when the enemy begins to lie most to us. At night, when the hospital was quiet and dark,

I would feel these lies of the enemy coming after me, saying, "You know, you're about the same age as your father when he took his own life in a psychiatric hospital. You're not going to make it out of here. You know, God is not with you. You're completely alone."

And so I would literally drag myself out of bed and plant my feet down in the middle of my bed in that little room in the psych hospital, and I would make this declaration over my own life. It was from a psalm that I believed to be true, whether I felt it to be true or not. This is what I declared over myself when I wanted to choose that, in Christ, no matter how I felt, I was victorious: *I would have lost heart unless I had believed that I would see the goodness of the Lord in the land of the living. Wait on the Lord, be of good courage, and He shall strengthen your heart. Wait, I say on the Lord.*

I knew my emotions were all over the place. But I realized emotions don't have brains. The word of God remains true no matter what I feel. So every night, I would choose victory over feeling like I was a victim. One night, I declared it so loudly that one of the nurses came to make sure that I wasn't seeing somebody in my room! I reassured her that all was well.

CG: *Did you see your choice to move from victim to victor as part of your calling and purpose?*

SW: I believe that every single one of us who loves Christ has a story. We can keep it to ourselves because we don't want to share the pain of it. There was a time when I wasn't sure I wanted to tell anyone I spent a month in a psych hospital and that I had a diagnosis of severe clinical depression. But then I began to realize, like Joseph said, every single thing the enemy intended for evil God intended for great good. Not just for Joseph, but for his people.

God will do a beautiful thing with a broken life … if you give Him all the pieces. Christ could have chosen to leave the marks of crucifixion behind in the tomb with the rags He was wrapped in, but He didn't. He chose to rise still carrying the marks of His crucifixion.

The only scars that will be visible in eternity will be the scars of Christ. When wounds are open, we need time for healing. But when they become scars, they become part of our calling and our purpose. Because where your scars are, there lies your authority.

CG: What advice can you give to others struggling with life's injustices?

SW: I think we tend to see life from a very human perspective in terms of thinking it should be fair. Often, we think nobody understands what we've struggled with or how much we have gone through. But Psalm 56 says that God does, and He has collected all our tears and recorded them in His book. Now, why would God do that? I think it's because He wants us to know nothing is wasted.

The ground is level before the cross. God doesn't care if you've ever written a book or spoken in public. But when we determine every day to get up and say, "Yes, Jesus, I'm all in," we move from being a victim to being an absolute victorious believer in Christ Jesus. And no one no one can touch that.

Introduction

You can win right now. The choice is yours.

Simply put, you can't walk in *victory* unless you choose to be a *victor*, and you can't choose to be a victor if you choose to be a *victim*!

I think that, when given the choice, all people would *choose* to be victors and not victims! The issues and confusion occur because so many people around the world don't *feel* they have a choice. They believe the lie that their skin is the wrong color, the pie isn't big enough, their neighborhood isn't nice enough, or their education isn't good enough. Sometimes, they even believe the lie that God doesn't care enough!

I also know many people who believe that, despite their best efforts, they just can't get a break! Because of things that have happened, the way friends and family have treated them, and often because of some lie or distorted truth they have been told, they blame the world around them for their inability to get ahead. That lie lives in their heads, incorrectly guiding their lives. *You're fat. You're not attractive. You're stupid. Nobody loves you.*

Those lies set up an *expectation* of failure. *If I am black, I'm not treated fairly because all white people are racists and have white privilege. If I am fat, they won't hire me because I am overweight. If I am a woman, they didn't pick me because I'm not a man. If I was successful, they would have included me or invited me.* Well, maybe. But, more often than not, these lies have replaced real *identity* with a *"victim's mentality."* They progress to a disease called *"poverty of the mind."* Try as they may, those with this disease live in a world of anger, disappointment, and blame. Worse still is the fact that the consequence of this disease kills generations of people and nations of citizens. That consequence is an expectation of failure in everything! It creates a paralyzing, sad lack of hope for anything good in your future—and it's against what God has planned for you in every way.

Maybe that's you! Maybe you too feel as if life dealt you a bad hand and it's the only one you get to play. Maybe in every job interview, every relationship, every area where you have a desire to have victory, you have unknowingly exalted a diseased expectation of failure. Even more tragic is the fact that this expectation is passed on to your children and to everyone around you who feels the weight of it. You feel as if you have no choice. The good news is that you do!

Sadly, the victimization of entire races and classes of people has become the political platform of choice to control us. Leaders today promote "victims" with no real solutions for their "victory," and political correctness has eliminated a dialogue that would honestly reveal much of what we refer to as "victimization" for what it really is: an inability to get *unstuck* from your broken past! Simply put, it is often preferable to keep you rooted in victimization than to see you set free from mental slavery.

Most people have experienced a lot that *is* wrong and *deserving* of blame. Life is unfair and bad things do happen to good people. In fact, some people do really bad things to other people, creating a ton of confusion and anger. The overwhelming amount of anger in the world today is evidence of wrongs that have piled up over time, causing a tremendous feeling of hopelessness and defeat for many people.

Tragically, over time, the anger of defeat feeds the "victim mentality," and generations of people become stuck. They are stuck in blame, stuck in anger, and ultimately stuck in defeat. They are stuck in a life as *victims*. Worse still, victims teach their children to be victims because, in sharing anger and pain with their children, they grow up with their parents' expectations of failure and defeat.

However, in everything, there is a choice to be made. And the incredible, beautiful choice to progress from victim to victor is one of the most important ones you can ever make.

But there are many things that war against *your choice* for victory and many "excuses" and "justifications" we all have to overcome in order to make it. I get this. I have been there. So have plenty other folks. Many have chosen to live as "victors" after making a conscious *choice* not to live defined by the things that victimized them.

Bill Gates's first business failed. Albert Einstein didn't speak until he was four years old. Jim Carrey was homeless. Bethany Hamilton had her arm bitten off by a shark. Richard Branson has dyslexia. Stephen King's first novel was rejected thirty times. Jay-Z came from extreme poverty and not one record label would sign him. William Paul Young, author of *The Shack*, was sexually abused by men between the ages of four and fourteen, and his book was rejected by every publishing company in the USA. People such as Denzel Washington, who has recreated dozens of roles initially written for white movie stars, and Nick Vujicic, who was born with no arms or legs, have overcome obstacles such as race, physical deformity, and "justified blame" for myriad reasons, to *choose* not to live as victims! While not all of these victory laps are run by believers, it is undoubtedly those whose *faith* allows them to experience the deeper healing found in Christ who ultimately walk in the greatest victory.

Failure is often misunderstood as a quality for the weak and doomed. Yet the circumstances which you may perceive to be the reason for your failures can turn out to be the driving forces behind your strength and your success. Simply put, victims blame circumstances for every failure. Victors use those circumstances as the palette for their success. Which will you be? Which do you *want* to be? I will say it again: the choice is yours!

Through much soul searching and education and after many years in ministry, I *know* there are transformative principles at work in *choosing victory*. In spite of your life circumstances or religious beliefs, these principles are incredibly powerful, incredibly real, and incredibly essential to living a successful life. In fact, these principles are so critical that our spiritual enemy is working hard to keep us from stepping into them. We'll talk about all of them in these pages so you can know what they are and how to apply them to become the victorious overcomer God has called you to be.

The poverty of the mind that has overtaken entire cultures of people around the world can only be defeated through a deeper understanding of our real identity as overcomers and children of God. Choosing not to live in blame, to walk in victory, and to live at peace is rooted in a daily choice to truly see the many things we have to be grateful for and the myriad possibilities that open up when the human spirit shifts from anger and blame to freedom and victory. A *victor* marches around the walls of his fears, his pains, his unmet expectations, and his own anger, and those walls must inevitably come tumbling down!

There is infinite power in understanding the vision of what you *can* be, and equally destructive power in the constant reminder of what you are not. The Bible states that for lack of vision, God's people perish. Have you ever really had a vision of the *more* that you were created for and not just the more that you want to have? If not, you are no doubt perishing along with millions of people around the world. You are shriveling up, getting older, losing your passion and *joi de vivre*, becoming someone you likely never set out to be. Seeing from God's point of view replaces our victimized perspective with vision for victory in spite of our circumstances, limitations, and setbacks.

The question you have to be asking by now is *how*?

How can I be powerful, resourceful, and faithful? How can I stare down the demons of my past, forgive those who've treated me wrongly, and move forward in a way that brings real success? How can I unburden myself from the root causes of my anger and blame in a way that helps me rise above circumstances, fears, hurt, and trauma? How can I truly move from living and thinking like a victim to living and thinking victoriously, no matter what socioeconomic environment I'm from, no matter what injustices I have experienced, and no matter what abuses I've suffered? How can I win? How can I choose victory?

We're about to answer all those questions. Come with me on a journey through three different war zones where battles must be successfully waged to get to the victory zone. It won't be easy, but nothing worth doing ever is. And believe me—moving from victimhood to the reality of a victorious, overcoming life is worth everything it takes to do it.

Yours in victory,
Cynthia Garrett
May 2020

PART I

The Personal War Zone

VICTIMOLOGY

I feel like a victim. I feel forgotten. I feel overlooked. I feel angry. I feel lost.

I feel like the best of life is behind me. I feel like I have no future. I feel like the future in front of me is all bad. I feel like I have no passion for anything. I feel unmotivated. I feel afraid. I feel sad. I feel like crying. I feel like God doesn't exist—and if He does, He doesn't exist for me. If He does exist for me, He is clearly punishing me, blocking me, and destroying the dreams I thought He gave me. I have served Him, yet I feel like He doesn't care. I am a Christian, yet I feel like I don't believe. I feel hopeless, and my tomorrows no longer seem inspiring to me. I feel like a loser! I am a victim and nobody cares.

I have felt every one of these emotions myself. In fact, we *feel* so many things through the days and seasons of our lives. There are many reasons for these feelings—some valid and some invalid. Yet one thing I know is true: victory doesn't live within your feelings. It lives within your *choices*.

You must *choose* victory! You must choose it till you see it, and even then, you must continue to choose it because your eyes may never see enough to prove to you that you actually are a winner!

Your victimology consists of a powerful network of feelings. Feelings form a deceptive place to live. Feelings cripple. Feelings rob. Feelings steal. Feelings destroy. Feelings lie. Feelings accuse. Feelings blame. Your victimology is Satan's strategic profile of you to keep you locked within your war zones, where how you *feel* is his greatest weapon.

As divisive as he may be, political commentator Ben Shapiro often says, "Facts don't care about your feelings." He's right. Certain feelings have zero to do with the facts of your gender, your finances, your education, your religion, where you were born, or when. Facts are no respecters of persons—not even when those facts place us on the unstable ground of our feelings.

What happens when you feel sad, or defeated, or different? What happens when you feel like the world is prejudiced against you because of the color of your skin or because of your gender? What happens when you feel as if you can't get ahead because you're poor? What happens when you experience very real feelings because of very real circumstances? Simply put, what happens when the facts are not your feelings, but your feelings exist *because* of the facts?

What happens is that you find yourself in a war zone. It's occurring inside you daily. And it's very real.

There are three key war zones where you will fight to move from victim to victor: the personal, the spiritual, and the political. No matter the outcome, we experience much pain and turmoil in these zones, and each is wrought with feelings, and they feed the fires that rage.

Feelings are tricky when you are fighting a battle within a particular war zone because feelings are connected to the heart—and trusting the heart is seldom advisable. In fact, the Bible says the heart of man is deceitfully wicked and who can know it? So how on earth can you trust the things your heart wants you to feel when your feelings exalt themselves against the reign of reason in your life every time?

Reason, knowledge, and wisdom are critical to choosing victory because your feelings will keep you in defeat. As a result, reason, knowledge, and wisdom are the first casualties of war. When you are choosing victory, your feelings are, in large part, your enemy.

One thing you must understand is that all three war zones are connected. Everything big is affected by the small. Significant things commonly are rooted in battles that seem insignificant. In your choice for victory, your smaller, personal life events and injustices actually drive the ferocity of your struggle in the seemingly bigger war zones.

The personal war zone we must fight in is the one that concerns our life experiences. A victory here is deeply connected to a victory in your spiritual war zone. In the same way, victory in the political war zone of an entire nation is critically impacted by its citizens' victories in the personal and spiritual war zones of their lives.

To be blunt, it's not about you—except in the personal war zone. There, it's *all* about you! It's about the injustices you've experienced, the pain you've endured, the anger you feel, the fear that drives you.

Choosing to be a victim in any zone will create a system of victimization in every other zone. When you are committed to moving from victim to victor, you will quickly find that victory is not a possibility or an option. Victory is a *choice*. Victory is the *only* choice. And it is your choice to make.

Your personal war zone is unique to you, but you are not unique in having one. We all do. For instance, I had trust issues for many years because of childhood betrayals and a foundation that I couldn't trust. I had intimacy issues because of childhood sexual abuse. If you can recognize the unique components of the injustices in your personal war zone, you'll have a tremendous ability to be victorious in life in general.

The change in the world really does begin with you. Your story affects all of us. Your fight against the circumstances of your story is epic in multiple war zones. This requires you to deal bravely with all the facts, components, and feelings that make you *you*!

Why? That's simple. Because *you* are the difference. When you choose victory, *everybody* wins.

Until you confront *you* and make choices based on healing your issues, which all relate to the things that have damaged you going back to your childhood, you will only effectively be choosing to remain broken. You will be choosing to stay stuck. You'll remain stuck in a cycle of victimization, producing nothing but victimizing results for yourself and anybody you love.

Seeing the Change

Recently, I had the chance to see how some of my choices are making a difference on another continent.

Last January, I went to India with a group on an awareness trip with an incredible organization called Opportunity International. OI is the oldest, most successful micro-finance organization in the world. (For those of you who don't know what micro-finance is, don't feel bad. Neither did I before OI.) OI makes small loans, averaging $189 apiece, to people, mostly women, living in the poorest regions of the world. These loans, incredibly, change lives and impact entire villages. They are based on the chief philosophy of my life and what it means to choose victory: a leg up and not a hand out!

My friends and I landed in New Delhi on a warm and smoggy day, with an itinerary set to meet OI clients in several villages, with some sightseeing and shopping in between. (Girls will be girls, after all.)

We journeyed by bus into regions that exist on the lowest levels of India's caste system. Villages where people live in extreme poverty. Villages where children have nothing. Villages where bathing and washing is still done in rivers and where a busload of American women arriving was something like the *Titanic* pulling into your local marina—it just doesn't happen.

Each village was home to a group of women who had each received loans from OI; the members help each other and keep each other accountable for repaying their loans. This accountability is all about victory in building a business as a means to make money—not only to assure their loans get repaid, but that their children get educated. Educating their children was by far the majority of these women's number one goal. They believed, as do I, that education is the key to ending the poverty cycle of their lives. These women live in tiny shacks with dirt floors, most with straw roofs, yet they are proud of the loans they'd taken to help them open various businesses. Some women opened snack stands. Some opened tailoring businesses by buying a sewing machine. Some women opened restaurants. Granted, these roadside businesses in their very poor villages don't look like your idea of restaurants and snack stands or tailoring businesses in the Western world, but they are successful and thriving, enabling these women to change their families' lives.

We got to celebrate "repayment day" with them. The women dressed up in their very bright, colorful wraps and saris and danced with us to celebrate making their loan payments on time. Monthly repayment is a grateful celebration of their choice to rise up in faith.

On one of those celebration days, I saw my own choice for victory on full display.

After a career in network TV, where I made a lot of money doing stupid entertainment shows, I launched a program that I executive produce called *The Sessions with Cynthia Garrett*, which airs on TBN internationally out of the UK and on the Cynthia Garrett Ministries YouTube Channel. It is seen by millions, but makes no money. I wanted to change people's lives and impact them with the truth of my faith, so I launched *The Sessions* to get women around the world dialoguing about how to really live life with faith. It's a "walk show" because I believe the world doesn't need just another talk show.

But one night in India, I stayed up fairly late, complaining to my friends Stephanie and Christine. I was lamenting the fact that I wasn't sure charity really helped. On that night in particular, I was feeling like the thing I was doing for all the right reasons wasn't really validated in terms I understand and can measure—i.e., money—so why do it? I felt like I was wasting my time and wondered if anybody really cared.

The next morning, we landed in the middle of nowhere in a place rarely, if ever, seen by American eyes.

We entered one of the small huts. The women had laid their only blankets on the dirt floor for us to sit on. They had smiles on their faces and were full of curiosity and wonder as they looked us over. We eyed them with the same curiosity and wonder at how beautifully dressed they were and how, in spite of their poverty and victimizing circumstances, they rose to a place of genteel hospitality, sharing the best they had, of the little they would ever have, with us.

I noticed how the women who had taken more than one loan—which meant they had successfully repaid a prior loan—walked and moved with more pride than the others. Essentially, the first-timers were still shy and insecure about their choice for victory. Such poverty and hopelessness all around you, year after year, brings tremendous insecurity and a lack of self-confidence. Yet in the women who had made and repaid loans once or more, I saw proof of how one small, shy, insecure choice for victory becomes an endless ripple in a pond of incredible transformational change for the better.

As we crowded as many in our group as we could into the small hut and sat down on the ground, the colorfully dressed women sat down as well. They whispered among themselves. Then one of the Indian women pointed at our group, saying in broken English, "You. Sister." Not sure who she was pointing to in our group, we all looked around.

"Sister. You." She pointed once again, locking eyes with me. I looked at her, unsure still of why she would single me out, and replied, "Me?"

She smiled. "Yes. Sister. You. We know who you are."

She and the other women giggled as they separated a little so I could see a tiny old television on a table behind them. It had cords and extensions running up through the straw roof into God knows where for power. In shock, I listened as she continued. "Sister, we know who you are. We watch you there. But what we want to know is how is it possible that God has brought you to my home?"

I burst into tears.

Wrecked with emotion as they watched me crying, my two girlfriends started to cry as well. Stephanie looked at me and said, "That was a gift from God for you."

I knew that it was. It was an echo of affirmation for the choice I had made long ago, and continue to make daily, to choose victory over the victimization my life had been riddled with.

There is often a lack of resources to fund the TV programs I pour my heart into to help women around the world walk out their faith. But I was being given the gift of seeing that my small choice to live in victory was reaching around the world into the remotest villages, across religious lines and cultural barriers, whispering hope into the lives of these women. My choice for victory had become part of their choice for victory. Every little bit does make a difference.

Every time you choose to rise above the limitations you live with, you are influencing humanity in ways you may not ever get to see. Trust me, those ways are there, and those influences are numerous.

YOUR
(VERY) PERSONAL
WAR ZONE

The deepest battle any of us will fight is the one within ourselves. It is the fight we wage with our own story. It is our personal war zone that we continually need to revisit until we experience the full freedom of our choice to move from victim to victor!

My own journey through this war zone has been an incredible battle, one in which choosing to play the victim certainly would have been easier. To be honest, choosing victory is still a daily battle. While life is beautiful, it is also hard. But not choosing victory is choosing to be defined by my experiences rather than by who God created me to be. Life is short, and I cannot afford to be defined by anything less than that! And whether you know it yet or not, neither can you. Nothing in God's definition of you includes the word "victim." There are many references to us as sons and daughters. We are called conquerors, overcomers, victorious, and loved. We are never called victims!

That force inside you that makes you want to fight the world to get ahead, to prove your point, or to simply win stems from your intuitive awareness that you were created for more than the cruddy circumstances you may have seen far too often in your personal story. *More* has many definitions and degrees, but there is a *more* that will give you the victory you desire. This is why many of us live in a war zone with personal realities that we inherently cannot and should not accept as God's will for our life.

Let's look at an example of this in the Word. In John 5, Jesus finds a man lying by a pool, where he and many others lay sick and diseased in various ways. The location was Bethesda, a supernatural site where an angel would come down and stir up the waters. When this angel arrived, the first person to jump in was healed of whatever disease they had. Talk about an amazing opportunity for instant healing! (We have opportunities to grab our healing more often than we recognize; that's why this story is important.)

Jesus walks up to this man, who has been afflicted with an infirmity for thirty-eight years. Thirty-eight years of being upset about the same injustice. Thirty-eight years of being angry about the same pain. Thirty-eight years with the same prayer and the same cry for help.

When Jesus saw him lying there, and knew that he already had been in that condition a long time, He said to him, "Do you want to be made well?" (John 5:6 NKJV)

The first thing we should conclude here is that Jesus knew this man hadn't been sick for just a week. His disease had gripped him for most of his life. Jesus surely knew that someone who has been sick for a long time can end up wrapping their identity around that sickness, and rightfully so. In short, what comes against us can become part of our identity, and even define it, if we are not discerning.

Jesus confronts the *victim mindset* right from the start. It may seem as though He is being a little harsh and uncaring, at least by our modern-day standards of political correctness: He doesn't ask why the man is sick, how he got that way, or who may be to blame. No intake is done at all to understand the *facts* that got him to this place. Jesus's question goes to the core of the man's heart and motivation. *"Do you want to be made well?"*

You have to be thinking, *This seems like the dumbest question in the world! Who would want to stay sick?* When I read this parable, I am answering the question for the man before he can even speak, "Yes! Yes! C'mon, man, just say yes! Healing is right in front of you. Get the miracle. Say yes. *Choose victory!*"

Instead, we hear the victimization narrative—the reasons, the excuses. They all come together to tell Jesus a story.

The sick man answered Him, Sir, I have no man to put me into the pool when the water is stirred up; but while I am coming, another steps down before me (John 5:7 NASB).

Jesus didn't ask that. He just needed a *yes* or *no* answer. The ever-present decision to choose victory would have yelled, "Yes, heal me now!" The problem is, if the man says yes, he becomes personally responsible for his victory choice. If he says no, he looks like a fool to everyone because only a fool would say, "No, I don't want victory." Instead, he gives a list of *reasons* why he hasn't been able to get into the pool. Victims are great at giving reasons because victims are full of excuses. They are usually justified, but they are excuses nonetheless. At a certain point, the excuses don't serve the bigger goal of getting in the water. So the question remains:

Do you really want healing?

Let's be honest, if the man really wanted to be healed, he could have paid someone or even bribed someone. *"Hey, buddy, next time the angel comes, I'll give you a thousand dollars if you run and shove me into those waters. I'll pay you back the second I am on my feet. I'll get a job and earn plenty of money to make it worth your while. Whatever it takes. Get me in the water!"* Instead, he was so defined by his personal story that his answer *was the story. His disease had spread to his mind where he had written a victim's story, unable to even think of a clever way to deal with his circumstances because he had developed poverty of the mind.*

My younger sister and I were sexually abused by our older half-brother when we were children. I wrote about that in my first book, *Prodigal Daughter: A Journey Home to Identity* (Spiritual Chick Publishing, 2016), but it likely became more widely known in late 2019. That's because my half-brother made a movie about our father's life called *The Banker,* which was slated for wide release last December. Apple pulled it from a film festival in late November after my sister and I protested that the co-producer was a child molester who had not told the truth about our family in the film; the company then delayed the theatrical release indefinitely and has said nothing about rescheduling its streaming debut, which was slated for this January.

But the victimization has continued because many people who knew nothing of the facts surrounding our story of sexual abuse simply got angry that my sister and I were "depriving" them of their "right" to be entertained. Nothing has caused feelings of continued abuse the way this ugliness—expressed by people unrelated to anything in my life—has. Yet, the interesting thing about choosing victory through all of this has been the simple reality that, while people around the world experience harsh realities and abuse daily, *wisdom* really is born of pain! Victory is born of a refusal to reside in it.

There were other victimizing circumstances I've had to rise above as well. I suffered through my parents' divorce. I was raped as a teenager, abused mentally and physically in my first marriage, divorced, spent a couple years on welfare and unemployment, lived as a single mom with my son, Christian, until he was fifteen, experienced sexual harassment and marginalization in various forms in virtually every job I have ever had in Hollywood, and have survived cancer!

I am also a woman of color who made it up the mountain of the entertainment industry to become the first African-American woman to host a network late-night show. At one time there was Jay, Conan, and me! We were the late-night lineup on NBC. Trust me, my mountain was an uphill climb filled with more than a few undeserved obstacles and a fair amount of intentionally inflicted distress.

I am quite open about the many reasons I have to point the finger of blame and shout the loudest in anger. Yet I am acutely aware of what a waste of time and energy allowing such negative emotions to define and control me would actually be. *Why* would I choose to focus on what tried to limit me when I can choose to focus on God, who created me without limits? Why would I let my pain narrative speak louder than my victory choice?

I have learned to *choose* to forget what is behind me and to press forward, toward my highest calling. When Jesus showed up and asked if I wanted to be healed I screamed, "Yes!" and ran as fast as I could toward victory. What did that victory look like? It looked like freedom in my mind from the voices screaming a narrative of defeat and hopelessness at me daily.

It's amazing how, when you're making that choice for victory and running toward whatever you have to do to obtain it, you no longer notice the shackles of your personal story fighting to keep you bound to it.

Race

Race is a huge issue within our personal war zones. Why? For starters, racism is real. People sometimes get treated unfairly based on the color of their skin. We all know this. Often, people don't even recognize their own racist thought processes. So when you are a minority, it's easy to speak from the loud narrative in your heart that says, "They did not choose me because of my race." You need only remember that slavery was justified through a misuse of Scripture to understand why it may be very difficult even for Christians who are black to let go of their race card.

If you are a person of color, fighting to choose victory may require a huge degree of battling. But the battle must be waged. Feeling as if the world is against you because of your skin color is a deceptive and powerful weapon formed against you. Only you can choose to eliminate the weapon because you are the one holding it.

Race has a long and negative narrative in our history. I can't imagine how grieved the God who created us all in His image must be by our treatment of others based on race. Yet still He is there to help us do exactly what is hardest—to choose to live as victors and not victims because He created our skin color and our differences as an expression of His perfection.

I learned firsthand how to journey from victim to victor in this area because my parents never allowed the circumstances of their lives to define them as victims.

My dad was black. My mom, from New Orleans, is Creole with a white face and very little black blood. She could have lived her life as a white person, as many in her family do and did. Their marriage was filled with challenges because of racism in the late 1950s and early '60s. Yet their choice to move from victim to victor included even the March on Washington with Martin Luther King. Part of an elite circle, they were proudly seated in the third row, center, when he made the speech that shook the nation.

Even as a child, I understood they lived through a lot of good and a lot of bad. However, because they didn't complain and tell me how unfair life was, my siblings and I never inherited poverty of the mind. We grew up knowing one simple thing: when life knocks you down, you get up. When life gives you lemons, you make lemonade. When life seems unfair, you figure out how to use the little you have and make more. The choice they showed me in their actions was always the choice for victory.

Through the early 1960s, my mom and dad amassed quite an empire. She and other close friends often served as his white face to get into board meetings for his own companies because he knew he would draw unwanted attention, jealousy, and even hatred because of his black face. He grew up with very little and worked his way into a real estate fortune, at one time owning half of downtown Los Angeles. Together, they began acquiring banks in Texas in the early '60s when blacks still couldn't ride at the front of the bus. My dad, Bernard Garrett Sr., and his business partner, Uncle Joe Morris, disguised themselves as a chauffeur and a janitor to get into their own banks.

I asked my dad once if having to do this ever made him angry. My dad laughed and said to me, "Slim, I didn't have time to be angry. I was too busy coming up with a way around how stupid it was to think I couldn't own a white bank because I was black. That's when I looked at your mama and Matt and had the idea to let them pretend to be the owners."

When politicians in Texas found out that two black men owned the banks, they were indicted on trumped-up bank fraud changes, and racism caused their banking empire to crumble. In response, my dad went back into real estate, where he always made money, and used it to build another empire in the Bahamas. Never one to choose defeat or to live from a place of victimization, I watched my dad get up over and over again until the day he died.

My mom is the same. Their eventual divorce after their adventures in the Bahamas was not easy for a woman with six children. Yet she rebuilt her life and remained friends with my father till the day we buried him. Even now, the unauthorized movie I mentioned in the previous chapter remains an issue, and at the time of this writing, my mom is trying to choose victory.

All of us, if not careful, can carry *a story* within us that is not *the* story God has given us. The story we carry can be littered with chapters of undeserved and unhealed pain, distorted perspectives, and limited thinking. We can carry that story into many different situations, projecting it onto future encounters. The man at the pool of Bethesda had a chance to address his story and replace it with the one Christ was bringing to him—a story of healing and wholeness.

It is the same story God is bringing to us today, but we have to ask ourselves the same question: *Do I really believe that moving from victim to victor, from sickness to healing, is my choice?*

I have sat down with many people who were looking for healing from a debilitating disease, a way of thinking, or anger about an issue in their life. They wanted to see if we could get to the root of what was holding them back and, in essence, pray it away. I have often felt horrible, asking them, "Do you really want victory in this area or over this issue?"

They look back at me like I am crazy. "Of course, I want victory in this area of my life! That's ridiculous!"

Then I say, "Well, are you willing to give up your disability check if you get healed and no longer need it? Are you willing to stop blaming the world and everyone you know for your problems? Are you willing to stop focusing on race and gender as the reason you've been passed over or mistreated, even if it was the reason?"

A moment of silence falls as they ponder how their problem has actually developed into a whole world of needed provisions that may be challenging to let go.

I am not trying to knock getting financial aid or medical help. I have had seasons of life when I received both. That is not the point here. I am getting to the root of whether or not you really want to be healed from having a victim's mindset because with healing comes responsibility for a new lifestyle and an entirely new way of living.

My mom and dad chose victory daily, even when racism presented obstacle after obstacle to creatively overcome. The focus of their energy was victory. Their mindset said victory. Their life mirrored victory. Even in victimization and moments of defeat, my parents chose to fight continually in the war zone created by their race and personal circumstances, never choosing to live from poverty of the mind.

What did their victory choice look like? It looked like try, try, try again. What did their victory choice sound like? It sounded like love, expressed to all people, because not all people of a certain race are good or bad. What does their victory legacy look like? Six children who all have careers and make decisions for themselves—four of whom have graduated college, one with a masters, and one with a law degree who is writing a book on choosing victory!

Class

My parents divorced when I was about thirteen. It wasn't easy to raise six kids alone, but my mom did it. It wasn't easy to educate all of us through college, and some through graduate school. We didn't have loads of money. But her victory narrative said, "This is the option you give your kids." Somehow, her choice for victory created a way. Somehow, yours will also.

My dad, ever the entrepreneur, experienced a lot and a little, so he couldn't always help financially. But rather than give money to attorneys, focusing on negativity (as is the case in most divorces), my mom accepted what my dad could do as he was able, and she did what she had to do when he couldn't. They focused on raising their kids victoriously. My life today looks very different than the circumstances in the very real war zone that would have told me I could never afford college, study in Europe, get a law degree at a top-ten university, or work in television and travel the world, speaking to millions from the platform God gives me daily as the reward for my victory choice.

The class system you grow up in is very connected to your exterior circumstances, so the war in the mind comes with a very real external enemy.

What do I mean? When you have no money, you feel it in your experiences every day. You know that *you* have less than *they* do. I remember being in high school and parking my first car, a beat-up old Dodge Dart, around the corner from school so none of my wealthier friends would see it. This may seem absurd, but you have to understand that I went to Beverly Hills High School; the other kids didn't drive normal cars. They drove nice new cars. My mom was single by the time I began high school, so there would be no new car for me until I worked and bought one in college. When you feel as if you cannot have what you desire (in my case, a new car), you either figure out how to work hard and get one, or you steal one, or you become hopeless, angry, and sometimes desperate. In myriad ways, we wrongly allow the presence, or lack, of *things* to define the class system we live in.

Oddly enough, I experienced both wealth and poverty, and the financial instability of my life created one of the greatest war zones for me to fight in. My parents, who achieved so much, also lost a lot. I graduated from USC Law School but chose a career in Hollywood, which sadly would serve to mirror the financial instability of my childhood. Since childhood, my greatest fears have centered around money—not having it—or having it and losing it.

The weapon I employ most in my personal war zone involving money is that I remember who I am. This is where those with faith have an edge over those who are not yet acquainted with their ever-present and long-waiting Savior. As a Daughter of the Most High God, I know that He loves me and will provide for me. *I know that I am to be anxious for nothing but to cast my cares upon Him. I know that He has good plans for my life, and*

I trust Him in faith. Why? Because I am His daughter. I am rooted in my identity.

This will seem like an insufficient answer to many, but whether you are a Christian or not, the only way to battle in a war zone of circumstances that tell you not only can you not afford to play the game but you will *never* be able to afford to play—and neither will your children or grandchildren—is to shut that voice down in faith and dig into the well of strength inside you that shouts back, "I can do all things through Christ who strengthens me!" Your faith, no matter what you think, is your ultimate weapon. You win the battles by knowing your identity.

Who are you in Christ, and who is Christ in you? The answer to these questions will constantly need clarifying because they will present themselves constantly in your fight to win in any of the war zones in your life. *But without faith it is impossible to please Him, for he who comes to God must believe that He is, and that He is a rewarder of those who diligently seek Him* (Hebrews 11:6 NKJV).

Whether you're a Christian or not, do you love yourself even though you were not born on top of the hill? Are you a good friend? A good parent? A good spouse? Do you have honor and integrity? The person you are is not determined by the class system you are born into. I know many bad wealthy people, and I know many great poor people. In fact, oftentimes, as we all know, wealth corrupts good character—and only when a person with much wealth realizes they cannot buy everything, such as good health, do they begin to deal with *who* they are rather than *what* they are and what they have. When you have fewer exterior trappings to hide behind, you deal with your inner self a lot more. Poverty and lack stretch you in ways that are incredible blessings if you choose to view things through a more productive lens.

Life has a way of leveling the playing field between the wealthy and the poor. My mom used to always say that in the end, it will be the "Haves" against the "Have-Nots." I look around constantly and see that she was right.

In fact, Jesus said, *"The poor you will have with you always"* (Matthew 26:11). In essence, there will always be "Have-Nots." This may seem unfair and harsh, but no matter how you feel about this fact, it's true.

You cannot regulate, adjudicate, or force equity amongst people. I would like to think we could regulate financial equity politically, but the effort will always be futile because it's not biblical. Moreover, people are not created to be the same. We are all equal, but we don't all have the same abilities. We are all significant, important, and powerful, yet we are all created uniquely and with different skills to ideally serve each other.

Try as we all may, I simply don't believe all things are created equal because they're not. I am not a man, and I am not as physically strong as my husband. In fact, women are typically physically weaker than men. To have us compete in this way is ignorant. Our society wants us to deny any differences between men and women. We are being asked to deny reason. Saying, "Hey, we are not equal here," is not mean or discriminatory. It's just an acknowledgement of the truth of how we are made. There is power in truth. Only truth will set you free.

I'm not talking about man's distorted, twisted truth; I am talking about the truth of what God made and honoring the power you find only when choosing to walk in His truth. The Bible affirms science all day long. That's why Planned Parenthood no longer argues that life doesn't begin at conception; it does. Science has proven it. We all know it. Now, Planned Parenthood is forced to argue for allowing murder based on the woman's life being more valuable than the child's.

Men and women should be treated equitably in ways in which we are created to have a level playing field—our brainpower, for example. Biologically, our brains have equal capacity and we should be treated, compensated, and celebrated equally. And while men may communicate love differently than women, we share equal capacity for loving and being loved. There are tons of ways in which men and women have the same components. However, to be ignorant of the ways in which one sex has something different than the other is to diminish the strength of what we have in common that merits equality.

Sadly, class, economics, and poverty have much to do with creating what I refer to as a "victim mentality." There are times in my own life when the weight of not getting the job because the network has already hired one black girl or because I had fewer financial resources than the next guy or because I didn't have the same opportunities growing up is really heavy to carry. There are times I can't believe I have to fight my way up from the ashes again. There are times when I wonder if I will ever achieve the things I desire. Times when I wonder, "Will life ever get easier?" Well, Jesus said, "*The poor you will have with you always.*"

So, I have come to understand that our response to this truth presents a deeply personal question that you may or may not wish to confront. *What if this is as good as it gets?*

Can we be content with our financial status, whatever that may be, while living joyously and working hard with only the *hope* for more? Can we live with a free mind and a joyful heart oozing our choice for victory no matter what? I've met homeless people with this spirit of victory on them, and I've met wealthy people with a victim's mindset and a constant victim's narrative. The latter is truly tiring for me to embrace. Circumstances have far less to do with this state of mind than the world would like us all to believe.

There are many neighborhoods, communities, people, and environments where living only with hope is not enough. Things are so bad day after day, year after year, that no matter what they have, or don't have, they simply can't see a way out. There are some who, tragically, have lost all hope.

POVERTY OF THE MIND AND WINNING YOUR MENTAL WAR

When there never seems to be enough and you never seem to have enough, a victim mentality settles in and spreads into a disease called poverty of the mind (POM). When entire communities are infected with a victim mentality, we often see a lack of motivation, misguided rage, hopelessness, blame, and many more symptoms of it.

POM is a direct result of the "victim mentality." It destroys the soul and stifles generations with an expectation of staying poor and never getting ahead. Once POM sets in, the battle to move from victim to victor intensifies because of expectations of failure and disappointment at every turn. POM establishes a comfort zone of sorts, a false reality, that life is *just this way*. Communities affected by this disease often continually set the stage for lack, with its guaranteed result of anger and uprising.

People become time bombs of rage when they feel they've been denied and deprived for far too long. Sadly, this occurs because the personal war zone created by unmet expectations, missed opportunities, and constant lack never goes away when individuals don't choose victory in the face of continual loss.

In African American communities, we used to have a greater foundation called the church. We had a stronger faith. We lived righteously before the Lord, and through fighting a better fight of faith, we achieved much in terms of freedom from slavery and establishing equal rights. Equal opportunity has led even to the presidency of the United States! Yes, it was hard, but life is hard. It took a lot of time, but time is relative. Our ancestors chose victory over victimization, rejecting the disease of POM, to rise up and sit in the place they knew their God-given identities had prepared for them. They made a choice.

Frederick Douglass made a choice. Rosa Parks made a choice. Martin Luther King made a choice. My father, Bernard Garrett Sr., made a choice. They chose victory. In spite of their circumstances, they chose to live as victors. This choice gave them the ability to press forward in victory, providing an example for all of us.

Imagine if they had chosen to live with a victim mentality, accepting POM as their lot in life?

Let's look at Frederick Douglass, an American social reformer, abolitionist, orator, writer, and statesman. He was born a slave in Maryland and never really knew his mother. After escaping from the plantation, he became a national leader of the abolitionist movement in Massachusetts and New York, gaining fame for his oratorical skills and incisive antislavery writings. In his time, he was described by abolitionists as a living counter-example to slaveholders' arguments that slaves lacked the intellectual capacity to function as independent American citizens. Northerners at the time found it hard to believe that such a great orator had once been a slave.

Douglass wrote several autobiographies and was influential in promoting abolition. After the Civil War, he supported women's suffrage and held several public offices. Though he didn't seek the office, he became the first African American nominated for vice president of the United States on the Equal Rights Party ticket.

Douglass was a firm believer in equality and constructive dialogue and believed strongly in making alliances across racial and ideological divides. When radical abolitionists, under the motto "No Union with Slaveholders," criticized his willingness to engage in dialogue with slave owners, he replied: "I would unite with anybody to do right and with nobody to do wrong."

Our nation would be completely different had Frederick Douglass not lived. He chose victory.

The Blame Game

There is often a bad guy in most injustices. Blame is often justified. Certainly, we all have many people and situations we can point the finger of blame at. However, when moving from victim to victor, blame is not only useless but completely unproductive. At some point, you must accept that *life* is no longer to blame.

Neither is God. Neither is your neighbor, your mom, your dad, your skin color, your economic background, your gender, or your education! Stop blaming everything and everybody. It's only *you* holding *you* down.

Blame gets you nowhere. Today, someone wasted thirty-five minutes of her life (and mine) yapping about what someone wrote in an email and how it wasn't her job to perform the requested task. She moaned about how offended she was and how little she was willing to do to fix the bad situation, because in her mind, she wasn't to blame for the situation at hand. In all honesty, she could have completed the requested task in less time than she spent blaming the person who sent the email. And this is just a minor example.

There are life circumstances that actually deserve your blame. I get that. I was sexually abused as a child and raped as a teen. There is clearly someone to blame in these situations. However, what happens after I point the finger of blame? I will tell you the answer: Nothing. Certainly, in some cases, there is prosecution. That's great. But in my case, with abuse that occurred as a child, the truth was suppressed for many years, and no legal recourse existed when it finally came out.

What about cancer survivors? Who do they blame? The doctors? Life? God? Themselves? It's not so clear in all situations where to place blame—but believe me, when something happens that you don't want to happen, you will scuffle to find someone or something to blame. It's human nature. *Someone* has to be wrong.

But what does it matter who's to blame? What does it matter who's wrong or who did what and who said what? What does it matter *how* I got cancer or *why* you didn't get the job?

Let me tell you; it doesn't matter. Blaming someone won't get you anywhere. It won't fix your circumstances. It won't heal you, deliver you, or set you free. Blame won't do anything except lock you in a prison of more blame. Blame paralyzes all forward movement while it revictimizes you over and over again.

Sadly, the victim often chooses to walk with *blame* as a constant companion. Yet when you walk with blame and a finger pointed at others, you'll often find yourself engaged in behavior that is deserving of blame as well. Those offended usually offend.

Those harmed usually harm. Those who are angry often lash out. The blame game is dangerous to play because when it comes right down to it, every single one of us could be blamed for something daily.

Luke 1:6 refers to Elizabeth (the cousin of Jesus's mother Mary) and Zacharias her husband, the parents of John the Baptist. They were two pretty important and righteous people, we can assume. I mean, it's not every day you get chosen to bear the child who will be the precursor to the Savior of the world and your cousin is chosen to bear the Savior. The Bible says, "Both of them were righteous in the sight of God, observing all the Lord's commands and decrees blamelessly" (Luke 1:6 NIV). That's pretty incredible. I, for one, am not blameless. I have done things that merit blame.

You have to ask yourself: *Who can stand before God without blame?* That answer is simple if you're honest: nobody. In fact, if we exercise a modicum of common sense, we know that "*all have sinned and fall short of the glory of God*" (Romans 3:23), except Jesus. Only Jesus had no blame. Yet, He died for all of us who do. When you can't *see* the sin in your life, you fall easily into the Blame Game. This occurs simply because we all want somebody, *anybody*, to be blamed when we feel unfairly treated.

Unfortunately, blame is often justified. We have to deal with that most important reality. There are people who do bad things, destructive things, and things worthy of blame. I have forgiven things that certainly were not worthy of forgiveness. (But more on that later. Forgiveness is too critical to relegate to a mere mention.)

The Blame Game also works in other ways. It hinders your success in other areas of your life, especially your profession. It's a ball and chain around your feet while you're trying to climb the mountain of success. When you're part of a team, it's tempting to want to shift the blame for failure off your own shoulders onto those of your colleagues or teammates. It's natural to want to attribute shortcomings to someone or something else. Instead of making excuses, however, start owning your actions. Instead of listing reasons why you can't achieve something, start taking actions toward achieving it. Start looking at *how* to be the solution, especially where a solution doesn't readily exist. That's what victors do. They make a choice to create victory, even on small scales, until they reach their bigger goals. Never is there room for blame when you are working on being your own solution.

No matter what the circumstances, you have control over your actions. Find a way to turn all your negatives into positives.

Winning Your Mental War

Isaiah 26:3 reads, *"You keep him in perfect peace whose mind is stayed on you, because he trusts in you"* (ESV). We have to learn to think differently so we can choose differently in order to live differently. But *how* do we *think* differently when we are engaged in a war in our own mind? This is a critical question! The answer is both simple and complex: You have to trust God. You have to take a very deep dive inside yourself and resolve once and for all whether God exists for you.

Why? Because faith truly enables the one making a choice for victory to live with a different peace than the person who chooses victory yet doesn't have faith. Faith is all about peace and the power to move forward.

There are many people who choose to live victoriously who do not have any faith whatsoever. They are not Christians, and they may not identify with any religion at all. They choose to live victoriously because they are motivated by pride in themselves and an inner drive they attribute to themselves. Perhaps they even have a sense of entitlement from skills they've honed. For these people, it's all about *them*. I get it.

I believed it was all about me for many, many years. In fact, it wasn't until I read the first sentence of Rick Warren's book, *The*

Purpose Driven Life, that that belief changed. The book opened with a simple statement on page one: "It's not about you." I almost had a mental breakdown! I had lived my entire life thinking it was about me. Me and my goals and my desires and my ability to get where I wanted or not. My education. My friends. My skill set. My hard work. It was most certainly all about me, and everything about my life affirmed that. I went to the right schools, traveled in the right circles, set the right goals, and did the right things. My parents told me I could do anything if I set my mind to it and worked hard enough. I didn't need God in that equation. I needed *me*.

Truth be told, I felt very alone and often completely over-whelmed by the reality that no matter how educated or attractive or connected I was, I felt deep inside that on most days I was not enough. My life and my success being about only me and my efforts was actually lonely and terrifying. While I looked as if I didn't need anything more than the fabulous me others could see on the out-side, on the inside, I was waging war with words that said I was far less than what they saw. *You were sexually abused, so you're unwanted and should carry shame. You aren't really smart enough. You don't know anybody in Hollywood, so how can you ever achieve your dream of working on TV? You're not as pretty as she is. You're not as smart as he is. If you were valuable, why did your relative molest you?*

All of the words associated with the facts of my personal back-ground often betrayed my sense of confidence. Therefore, I certainly didn't really believe I was *enough* to do whatever I desired. I some-how knew, like many of you do, that no matter how stacked the deck is in your favor, there is something bigger and greater than you. Honestly, in the years before reading Warren's book, I often felt totally afraid of the fact that I knew I was human and made mistakes, so I questioned daily what would happen to me and my son, Christian, if my mistakes caused me to fail.

Incredible freedom came in actually letting go and realizing that not only was it not about me but that God had incredible plans for my life and I was not alone! In fact, I was connected to a larger body of believers. I've come to know that we are all caught up in a story in which God's hand is moving through each of us and our different backgrounds. I see the tapestry of how we all function, woven together and working in beautiful harmony to achieve the plans of the Grand Master of the opera we are part of. This knowledge was, and still is, incredible to me. I no longer worry in the same way about myself, my son, or my life because I can see God's promises being delivered constantly as I choose the victory of trusting Him in the personal war zone where I fight my most intense battles.

Let go. Trust Him. Your first choice in choosing victory is choosing Him. You can choose victory without Him, yet you can only really *experience* victory in all its fullness when you choose Him.

We believers have the same pride and entitlement as non-believers, but our pride is centered in what our Father can do, and we are entitled because we are His children. As His kids, we can expect Him to be exactly who His Word says He will be.

He made me to go from victory to victory. He made you exactly the same, whether you believe that today or not. The knowledge of Him feeds my faith in Him, and my faith in Him feeds my trust in Him. My trust in Him allows me to see Him at work in and through me in all things. Whatever it is, I have peace that He will do it. I know I am capable and that no matter what I don't have or can't get, He can enable me to do all that I hope for. In fact, He will do abundantly more than I can dream or imagine, which means I will do abundantly more than I can dream or imagine because He is at work in me.

When you choose Jesus Christ as your Savior, your victory in the mental war you wage with words and thoughts that seek to poison your life is your assured inheritance. Life shows us that when we fight against the mental brokenness and traumatic experiences of our past, we need a Savior to emerge victoriously. The peace you receive in exchange for your choice of Him is a peace that surpasses human understanding. I have rested in it time after time after time. I encourage you to do so as well.

The War on Fear

Franklin Roosevelt assured people that "the only thing we have to fear is fear itself." The Bible makes an even bolder promise: We have nothing to fear—period.

However, when fighting in our personal war zones, let me tell you the only thing to fear is *everything* we have ever been through! You probably already know that everything you have been through makes you fear everything you *haven't* been through, too. But odds are you'll never experience even half of what you are afraid of.

In your personal war zone, *fear* is one of the greatest foes you will face! Fear is, in fact, the opposite of faith. The victim lives in fear. The victor learns to defeat it.

While Christians struggle with fear for a variety of reasons, if you live with fear, you are most assuredly living *without* faith. Fear is a huge participant and motivator of everything that wages war in our minds. In spite of your *best* fight, fear will work against your *choice* to walk in victory constantly! That's why you cannot be controlled by it.

I have learned how to speak the truth out loud to my fears because nothing combats the lies that our fears tell us like the truth of God's Word. I once said, "God has not given me a spirit of fear, but of power and of love and of a sound mind" (2 Timothy 1:7) at least ten times a day. Not joking. I was battling fear in a way I had *never* experienced. While it was irrational, it was getting the best of me. I have so much faith in the truth of this scripture because I have spoken it out loud every time I wrestled with fear, and the truth of it always defeats the lies of my fears. This scripture is my sword, and I use it to defeat fear constantly.

For a lot of folks, life provides plenty of reasons to live in fear. *I didn't get the promotion last time. He cheated on me before. I am poor. I don't know the right people. I am not the right color. I didn't go to the right school.* Poverty, lack, and hopelessness affirm the voices in your head bringing fear for the future, fear that you'll never make it, you'll never be able to do it, or you'll never win.

The Bible tells us *hundreds* of times not to be afraid. Why so many times? Because any force that is the opposite of faith, that can effectively kill faith, is worth being clear about. We need to know God does not want us to live in fear. He wants us to live in faith. Let me say that in victory terms: God doesn't want us to live as victims. He wants us to live as victors. Faith is a choice for victory. Fear is a choice for the victim.

That said, fear is rampant. I once made an altar call for prayer about fear in South Africa, and thousands of people came forward seeking freedom from it. *Thousands.* There were more people at the altar desperate for prayer to be rid of fear than most churches have members. So many came that the lines were backed up the staircases. Yet consider this truth. Isaiah 43:1 says "Don't fear, for I have redeemed you; I have called you by name; you are mine" (CEB). God knows the enemy uses fear to decrease our hope and limit our victories.

I've always struggled with fear. For as long as I can remember, there wasn't a molehill I couldn't turn into Mount Everest. My husband even nicknamed me Aunt Josephine, after the character played by Meryl Streep in *Lemony Snicket's A Series of Unfortunate Events.* In short, after three young siblings are orphaned, they are carted off to live with their distant relative, Count Olaf (Jim Carrey). Unfortunately, Olaf is a cruel, scheming man only after the inheritance that the eldest child, Violet (Emily Browning), is set to receive. The children escape and find shelter with their quirky Uncle Monty (Billy Connolly) and, subsequently, their phobic Aunt Josephine (Meryl Streep), but Olaf is never far behind.

Fear constantly pursues the children and in a hilarious illustration of how phobic fear can turn lives upside down, we see one of Meryl Streep's best performances ever.

Aunt Josephine, a widow who once was a great adventuress, is afraid of her own shadow. Her house, perched perilously on a cliff, is always cold because she's worried the radiator might explode; she doesn't want the children to get near the refrigerator because she frets it could topple and crush them; and she refuses to use the telephone for fear of being electrocuted. And don't even mention the giant, hungry leeches that surely live in the sea below her house.

While hysterically funny, Josephine is tragically sad. She is a victim of her own fears in the worst way. Rather than making the choice to live in faith and actually enjoy her lovely little cottage with the incredible view above the ocean, Aunt Josephine has chosen to be a victim to every fear she can imagine.

My husband made me watch this movie one day after telling me about it for two years. I will admit that while I laughed, I became upset. I realized how tragic Aunt Josephine really was, and I did not want to be her. On the outside, I was carefree and filled with faith. I was never afraid to go for it, whatever *it* was. Yet the girl my husband really knew on the inside was filled with fear, and it was the most intense battle in my personal war zone because many of the facts of my life had provided reasons for me to justify my fears. I cried watching the movie because I knew that in order to fully experience moving from victim to victor, I had to win the fight against fear.

The thing I liked least about Aunt Josephine's reality, which mirrored mine, was that just as she placed fear on the orphaned children, I had saddled my own son with a mountain of fears. He was my life. Fear was my foe. So losing him was the target of my fears. Consequently, I painted every scenario in his life with the clear danger zone of death. "Don't run up the stairs: you might fall and tumble down and break your neck and die." "Don't play basketball in the street—a car might hit you and kill you." Every new freckle dubiously resembled skin cancer. I was a single mom for fifteen years, so every new friend might be the one who introduced him to drugs and caused a fatal overdose.

Allowing my fears to be a song I sang over Christian in many ways was a horrible mistake that I am pleased I have seen the victory over—yet what a journey! You may be laughing, because it's hysterical when I recount all of this. But let me tell you that when I say I went to war against fear, believe me—I went to *war* against fear.

I learned that whenever things get too bad and your fears are screaming at you, remind yourself that the most common command in the Bible is *"Fear not,"* and start quoting Scripture out loud.

Why out loud? Because the *rhema* word of God is the sword of the Spirit Ephesians 6 refers to. *Rhema* means "spoken aloud." This is how we fight. The *rhema* word is part of a soldier's gear, and when we go into battle, we need to suit up correctly and carry the proper weapons. No soldier goes into a war zone dressed in shorts and a T-shirt, carrying a plastic fork to fight with. He or she wears armor suited for battle. Pick up your sword and fight.

Fear is a complicated emotion. It can sometimes motivate us, but more often than not, it paralyzes us. As Christians, once we allow fear to dominate our lives, we stop progressing. We stop living. This paralysis thwarts the calling you have on your life, the blessings of victory God wants to bestow on you, and the abundance of joy that comes from being thankful for another day rather than fearing it.

Yet how do we choose faith over fear? Simple: we press into God. We press into His Word. We combat the lies our fears bring with the truths that God brings. Fear is always about lies. Faith is always about truth. With the promises of God as our evidence, we can win daily if we simply keep choosing the victory of faith.

Sadly, we often exalt the god of lies and confusion rather than the God of truth and peace. In all honesty, Aunt Josephine, like me, made covenant after daily covenant with her mouth in agreement with her fears and Satan's lies. *Going for this job will only end in heartache because they will not hire me because I never get hired.* That simple agreement out of my mouth, coupled with the apparent lie that anybody besides God is responsible for promotion, gives the enemy enough to stop me from going for my dreams. In its own way, fear can become an idol that takes our focus away from God and leaves us to fret over "what if?"

Besides speaking Scripture out loud, how else can we combat our fears?

Many fears are born from a desire to control the outcome rather than trusting in obedience to God. In this scenario, you don't want to get your heart broken by going for yet another job—so you don't apply. It's uncomfortable for many of us control freaks to actually let go and let God be in control of our outcomes and of us. But in your choice for victory, you have to do just that. He has a plan. Your fear is likely that you won't like His plan or that you have to do something to further His plan to make it happen in your timing. Our timing, of course, is always *now*. His is not. This is scary. Not knowing what tomorrow may bring is enough to make anybody afraid, especially when we have lived through some pretty awful yesterdays. But no matter how "on lock" we think we have our tomorrows, we honestly don't have a clue what they will bring. Only God does.

Once you realize how integral faith is to your ability to choose victory, you learn the next big weapon to fight fear: Obedience. It's critical.

Obedience isn't control. When you follow Christ, you are to let Him be sovereign over the outcome of your obedience. Yet I know many who struggle with wanting to know what will happen before they obey. They want to know if their victory is assured before they choose to be obedient to the God who brings the victory. But we just can't know! Knowing isn't trusting, and victory requires trust.

In John 21, Jesus also told Peter about his future, saying, "Very truly I tell you, when you were younger you dressed yourself and went where you wanted; but when you are old you will stretch out your hands, and someone else will dress you and lead you where you do not want to go" (John 21:18 NIV). Following Jesus leads us to opportunities to choose to surrender more control of our lives each day. But surrender is never easy.

The Bible is filled with examples of individuals who are called by God to perform services they are reluctant to take on. One of the most prominent is Gideon.

Gideon is often considered to be the poster boy for fear. When God first commanded him to rescue the Israelites, he was hiding in a winepress to escape his enemies (Judges 6:11).

Throughout this story, Gideon lived in fear, anxiety, and doubt. He constantly tested God by asking Him to perform signs. First, he had God consume an offering of food he presented to an angel (Judges 6:20–21). Next, he petitioned God to send morning dew specifically on a piece of fleece he laid out (Judges 6:37–38). Finally, just for good measure, he lay out the fleece again but asked *for the exact opposite to happen* (Judges 6:39–40)!

Gideon was afraid, but when he finally put his trust in God and obeyed, the Israelites were freed from seven years of oppression. There will always be moments in life when we are worried about giving ourselves over to God, but the truth is we can trust Him with our tomorrows. Obedience does not require us to be fearless; it only asks that we have the faith to follow God in difficult times.

One of my favorite Christian writers, Corrie ten Boom, said it best when she wrote, *"Never be afraid to trust an unknown future to a known God."*

Do you know Him? That can be a big question in a world where contemporary Christians, even leaders, don't study their Bibles nearly enough—and sometimes not at all. I will go so far as to say that you cannot know God if you never hang out with Him and talk with or listen to Him. It's just not possible to know Him, or anyone, absent a personal, daily relationship where you spend time together as friends. This is the only way you'll overcome fear. It's the only way to no longer be a slave to fear, which holds you hostage to crippling emotions. Fear robs you of your ability to make the journey from victim to victor.

I use the song "No Longer Slaves" by Jonathan David Helser and his wife Melissa as the opening of my *Sessions* TV series because, to me, the greatest shout of victory I ever had was when I was given the platform to make the show I always wanted to make, talking about the only subject that matters: God and faith. "Is He real or not?" is the most important question you can ask on earth. That song is an epic cry of victory over fear. It is the ultimate song of joy over your life. We are no longer slaves to fear because we are children of God. We are the sons and the daughters, and we have inheritances promised to us, if only we can crawl to the choice for victory over fear. That victory is your faith. If you don't have it, the journey to victory over fear may never end.

BROKENNESS

Why is the personal war zone of our lives so difficult to fight in effectively? Why do we face so many mental battles here?

In a word, brokenness. Most of us are broken by our experiences. Until we understand what brokenness is and how it affects us, it's nearly impossible to find the freedom to choose victory. Our brokenness makes us see ourselves as victims, causes us to live in fear, and speaks lies about our identity.

I am an ordained minister of the Gospel. In fact, I am ordained to the PlanetShakers movement and to the International Federation of Christian Churches. I say this so you understand that, on a theological level, my husband and I have counseled others in this fascinating area for many years now. Brokenness results from past trauma that has created a fracture in the mind, body, and soul, called a "stronghold." The result: a broken heart that drives everything you do. Emotions lead while rational, godly reasoning goes out the window.

To set the stage, you'll first need to surrender. If you've chosen Jesus Christ as Savior and Lord, then surrender is a critical weapon in your personal war zone. I know that sounds odd. *How does one surrender and fight at the same time?* I don't mean surrender to your enemy, which is all the circumstances that created your personal war zone in the first place. I mean surrender to your *faith*. Choosing victory requires you to surrender to the faith you've chosen and let it be your ultimate weapon in life. This is why Christians should always find it easiest to never live with a victim's mentality— we have faith in a supernatural God.

Years ago, when Roger and I were engaged, I was complaining to him about my son's teenage angst and my fears for him as an unsaved boy in the New York-to-Hollywood community of uber-privilege in which I had raised him. I knew the reality was that my brokenness had caused me not to raise Christian the way I knew I should have. Because of that, I was afraid I was going to lose him and that I was going to pass a victim's baton to him because I had based his worth in *things* and not in his godly identity. I surrendered much when I began to pursue a relationship with Christ, yet back then, I was afraid it was too late to undo the damage I had done to my son by focusing for so long on a life of privilege, excess, and red carpets.

On top of that, I was moody and always felt unsettled, even though I had lived as a Christian for years by that point. I knew I wasn't experiencing honest freedom, and this was causing me to struggle with my faith.

In retrospect, I was saved in mountaintop spiritual experiences. I found Jesus in a prison in Italy where angels spoke to me, accompanied by dreams and visions. I have one of those huge cinematic testimonies filled with all the requirements that made my first book, *Prodigal Daughter*, epic to many who read it. I escaped from prison and returned to the United States, where I spent years on red carpets with privileges and access most people in the world will never experience. Then-President Silvio Berluscone's administration in Italy absolved me of any wrongdoing. Miracles.

Yet all I could do that day was look at my fiancé, knowing I didn't understand a thing about how to be free from the emotional pain I still felt inside.

"I'm a Christian. I go to church twice a week. I love people. I treat others well, and I speak about my faith all the time. But I don't get it," I told Roger as I cried deeply. "I've gone to therapy. I have the tools to recognize when my issues are kicking in, but why do I never get deliverance from the issues themselves? Is that all I get—tools to *cope*?"

Roger looked at me intently. He truly understood the depth of my despair and the point of my questions.

"I don't understand," I continued. "Why bother being a Christian? What's the point? I have everything I dreamed of having as a little girl on the wrong side of the block. I speak to others all the time about His peace, His joy, and why we need Him, but I don't have any peace or deep inner joy myself. I still hurt, and worse, I now expect that even with everything in my life going well, another shoe will drop and everything, including you, will go away."

Roger tried to interrupt me as I sobbed hysterically, but he couldn't interject a word.

"Where is my peace that surpasses understanding, Roger? Where is the abundance I'm promised in the Bible? If God is good and He is real, then is this *all* His *kids* get? Secular tools, from secular therapists, to *cope* with? Emotions control my day! I wake up in a bad mood some days. I wake up sad and down some days. Some days I wake up agitated and annoyed and fearful. My son and I fight like cats and dogs all the time! I don't get it, Roger. I must be broken beyond repair. Maybe this *is* all I get. And if that's the case, why am I *hoping* in God and a bunch of seemingly empty, or untrue, promises in the *Bible*? I *am* a victim. I want to quit. I am exhausted. I. Give. Up."

I came unglued. My faith came unglued. My life was coming unglued from the inside out. I was over it. I was over everything around me—the famous friends whose friendship I questioned constantly because I gave more than they were capable of returning; the career pursuits that never filled the void; and the fact that I feared I was losing the only thing in my life that mattered: my baby boy. I was over the fake, the phony, the shallow, the numbing, the superficial. Over it all.

All I could do was cry. I was so desperate to know how to *choose* a victorious life, yet I didn't have a clue as to how. I cried. And cried. And cried. I will never forget that time in my life because it was when I learned about my own personal war zone and the brokenness it caused.

Roger held me, consoled me, and began an explanation that would change my life. His explanation fuels the fire that rages in me to never again live as a victim but to choose victory daily. He explained to me what brokenness is and how to find healing. He opened the book of Isaiah and read from the beginning what Jesus proclaimed about Himself:

> The Spirit of the Lord is upon Me,
> Because He has anointed Me
> To preach the gospel to the poor;
> He has sent Me to heal the broken-hearted,
> To proclaim liberty to the captives,
> And recovery of sight to the blind,
> To set at liberty those who are oppressed ...

I've seen several miracles of healing since experiencing my own. While Christian was in college at the University of Kansas, he and his friends prayed for a deaf kid after a Bible study we hosted in our home one night. The young man, Jose, had already had five surgeries with doctors from Yale to Harvard, and nothing had worked—until that night, when God opened his ears. Years later, he's still sharing the Gospel. Countless college kids who came in and out of study, many of them student athletes, all received healings and other small miracles on a regular basis. Rock Chalk Jayhawk!

But nothing touches me like an emotional healing, which, in my opinion, is often far greater than the physical ones. The enormity of a child of God being healed of fear, anxiety, depression, anger, blame, or abandonment issues is equally as powerful and life transformative as those healed from physical impairments. While the physical impacts the body's ability to function at its highest level, much can be said about the emotional wounds and scars that impact the mind's ability to do the same. Emotional wounds are seldom visible. All we see are their consequences expressed in actions, bad choices, and derailed lives.

Brokenness caused by traumatic events, usually during child-hood, can mentally debilitate an entire life. Worse, broken people break other people. So the broken parts you carry threaten to damage not just you, but everyone around you—especially your kids. This is how legacies of sexual abuse, alcoholism, or financial debt are passed along from one generation to the next. Brokenness is a cycle.

Sadly, the church seldom fully comprehends the depths of this area. Yet it's why millions of Christians live feeling anything but peace that surpasses understanding, joy unspeakable, or the abundance promised by God. Millions of people around the world spend money daily seeking help. I sure did. They pay for therapists, psychologists, psychiatrists, gurus, psychics, healers, shamans, drugs, sex, fame—you name it. *Anything* for freedom from their emotional captivity. Some understand *why* they're in emotional captivity—but understanding the roots of the problem doesn't make it go away.

Secular therapy can give you all the tools in the world, and psychotherapy can give you pills, but there is only one power I have ever encountered that has completely set me free from the emotional captivity of my brokenness. I am not saying that some people don't need medication. I *am* saying that I have seen people come off medication once Jesus permanently heals them.

He promised us in Isaiah 61 that He came to bind up the brokenhearted and to set the captives free. Nobody else. Only Him. He gave power in His name to do many things, including cast out demons. But He reserved the power to bind up broken hearts and set captives free from their captivity for Himself.

When the heart and mind are broken, the damage is usually visible on the outside, even if misunderstood on the inside. Therefore, it is often made worse by the judgments, condemnations, and wounds inflicted by others and one's self. Why? Because people fight back when your brokenness fuels behavior others need to protect themselves from. People don't want to be around broken people because their behavior will at some point show itself as erratic, unpredictable, unsafe, and scary. While ignorance can be bliss, it really isn't in terms of brokenness. You need to recognize yours and get help.

God seems to allow things to intensify over time so that our brokenness becomes more obvious. For example, you become aware that normal people might become angry for normal things, but you go from anger to rage in the time most others take to become simply annoyed or agitated. With enough situations, you begin to suspect that perhaps you overreact, but you can't control it when the emotion comes on. People driven by broken emotions cannot build a successful life, hold a good job, keep good friends, forgive others, or see the world as safe enough to ever choose victory. They become stuck in a cycle of victimization, with blame and usually anger as their best friends. Poverty of the mind decreases any expectations they have for a better life, and in their brokenness and hopelessness, they raise their children to expect the same in return.

People who've never been broken experience a normal range of emotional expression. However, when you're broken you become aware that your insecurity, neediness, fear of rejection, or inability to sleep is fueled by something that doesn't seem quite within the normal range of controllable emotions. You lose control in an emotional part. When the part goes back into hiding, you're fine. When it comes out to drive the car of your life, you're racing down a speedway, headed toward a brick wall once again. And God help anybody standing in front of your car.

Some kinds of brokenness are more obvious than others. For example, kids who've been sexually abused typically break during the event and can react in a number of ways. My husband counseled one man who was sexually abused as a little boy, so as an adult, he used to wear women's underwear to be near something feminine. When his wife was around, he was fine—no female undies needed. But when he was alone—on a business trip, for example—and the memories would resurface, he would resort to the only method he knew to cope with his fear and feelings of shame. Out came the underwear.

Victims of sexual abuses can become sexually promiscuous, develop intimacy issues, or struggle with same-sex attractions. I've seen some women withhold sex or deny their femininity completely by dressing down or becoming overweight, so as not to draw male attention to themselves. Some men will hate women. Some women will be so angry with men that they treat them with disdain or belittle them. Both have a difficult time trusting and receiving love.

Imagine being in a relationship with someone with this type of brokenness. The love they desire they will literally sabotage, time after time. One young woman I knew took on the spirit of the boy that molested her as a little girl, and from the day of her abuse, her mom described her as *changing* and becoming more like a boy. In fact, she began dressing like the boy who molested her. Eventually, she expressed attraction to women, and whenever she and I speak of her being with a guy, she cries. She becomes the little five-year-old girl all over again. She is stuck in a broken emotion and in deep need of inner healing. God actually told me in prayer one day that the guy who abused her was, in effect, abusing more women each time she was with them because of the spirit of this guy that she took on. When I told her, she cried deeply and told me that she completely understood but that now she was who she *chose* to be. She never had a *choice* but she doesn't realize it, because her identity is now intertwined with her lifestyle behavior.

Another woman my husband and I counseled was the victim of a serial rapist. She came to us two years after the ordeal because she was experiencing fear and an inability to sleep. We, of course, thought it was some delayed reaction to the rape. However, knowing it's not us but God who must speak in an inner healing session, we simply prayed and kept quiet, and let God speak to His daughter. We were amazed when the memory that came to her was of seeing her puppy dart into the street and nearly get hit by a car when she was a small girl. Her fear part had initially broken as a little girl for her puppy, not from her rape. This explained why she kept saying she didn't experience feelings of fear at all during the actual rape, even while hog-tied in a shower for hours. The part that was created to deal with fear had long been there and went to work protecting her from experiencing fear during the rape. When this part got healed, she stopped experiencing fear in general and started sleeping peacefully through the night again.

Many cases are not about sexual abuse and extreme trauma, of course. Situations where the initial trauma is far less can be just as destructive and intrusive in a person's life. We prayed with a man whom God had revealed was riddled with *anxiety* because a parent left him in the car while she went inside the grocery store. This caused an inability to sleep peacefully as an adult. Once healed, he reported sleeping a solid eight hours a night from that day forward!

Another person had brokenness around never hearing her dad say he loved her. In that prayer session, she forgave her dad and got healed of feelings of low self-worth because of it. Not even twenty minutes later, her father called out of the blue and said he really felt awful suddenly and that he just wanted her to know he loved her. He even apologized for never telling her as a child. Now that's God!

Consequently, when people confront their brokenness, some often miraculously lose weight. They run marathons, they become clear about their sexuality, they achieve things they only dreamed of. Most importantly, many learn to love themselves for the first time in their lives.

INNER HEALING

You may be wondering what to do about all these things! Although you would like to shake the emotional parasite called "the victim mentality" and choose victory, you likely comprehend little about how to heal your own emotional brokenness.

This is when we turn deeper into Isaiah 61. I call this truly good news for the oppressed and broken!

He has sent me to comfort the brokenhearted and to proclaim that captives will be released and prisoners will be freed (Isaiah 61:1b NLT).

The heart is the seat of the soul. It's the center of all emotions. The soul is your personality, the person God made you to be. When the heart is broken, it affects your personality. This is why many people don't *feel* like victors. They *feel* like losers. You just can't be the amazing and successful *you* God created you to be when your heart is broken.

When your heart is broken by an event, you wall up emotions and set them aside to cope with the day to day. Emotional brokenness leads to manifestations of behavior that are usually completely irrational and often ungodly. This can look like rebellion and sin to the world. So you're judged and condemned, and more pain and brokenness is heaped on top of you, because now you're hurt by being judged and condemned by people. (Gotta love the church! The only place that shoots its own wounded with zero comprehension as to why they're wounded at all.)

God alone knows and judges the heart. This is why many times, blessing and covering continue to come to people you might otherwise judge as sinful and rebellious. Ahhhh. This is a big one. Pay attention.

Only God is qualified to judge a person's heart because He is a good Father who understands the emotional wounds, injury, damage, and pain His children live with, usually unsuccessfully. Since His mercies endure forever, as does His love, I am so grateful He chose to cover me, bless me, sustain me, and provide for me while I figured out I needed inner healing. Being set free from the captivity of my broken emotional parts allowed me to return home to Him and to find my identity as determined by *Him*. It freed me to choose to live my life from the standpoint of being victorious rather than from being a victim. Even though I have been victimized by circumstances and people, I am able to choose victory because my brokenness has been healed so that emotions like anger, blame, lack of faith, powerlessness, etc. no longer control me.

God never gave up. Yes, He saw the messes and mistakes and many times the rebellion the world saw. But He alone also saw the limitations, the wounds, the breaks, and the tears inflicted upon His child that had caused her to choose to live and behave way beneath her calling. As any good parent, He chose to guide patiently, lead mercifully, and rebuke gently. He never acted or spoke without love. And He never stopped pursuing me with love. Love never fails. Ever.

No matter what your life today looks like, His love never fails. He alone understands your brokenness like nobody else can or ever will. He desires to heal you from the emotional captivity your past holds you in, and He is not limited by human constraints in doing so. His is a supernatural healing. He, the same Savior who died for your sins, personally promises it.

No matter how big or how small, most people seem to have some kind of situation, usually in childhood, that has caused brokenness. That brokenness creates wounds that get fortified into strongholds. A stronghold is a fortress. It's a place you can run to that, over time, becomes more and more unhealthy. And God wants us running to Him alone.

Destroying these strongholds is something God cared enough about to discuss in the Bible. We are taught that *"though we walk in the flesh, we do not war according to the flesh, for the weapons of our warfare are not of the flesh, but divinely powerful for the destruction of fortresses [strongholds]"* (2 Corinthians 10:3–4 NASB). This is powerful. God is explaining that *"we are human, but we don't wage war as humans do. We use God's mighty weapons, not worldly weapons, to knock down the strongholds of human reasoning and to destroy false arguments"* (2 Corinthians 10:3–4 NLT).

The weapons we fight with are not of this world. They are spiritual. They have divine power to destroy strongholds. We don't have to do it ourselves because we have spiritual weapons to do it for us. But you have to know what the weapons are and how to use them. When you begin to use them, you begin to easily choose victory.

Prayer. Faith. The Word of God. Forgiveness. These are your weapons.

Most people, even leaders, don't understand the weapons of our warfare or how to use them to cast down strongholds.

Leaders themselves are often broken and are leading from brokenness on the pulpit. Strongholds can run our lives completely. They take us captive emotionally and can drive every decision we make. I dare say that you shouldn't desire to lead until you've confronted your own brokenness with inner healing. Why? Because if you do not, you are simply one prideful, gossip-filled scandal away from falling down. You have to go to battle spiritually to tear your strongholds down. Your flock depends on you!

Inner healing teaches you about the battle process. It's where you acquire many incredible tools to fight against the personal facts that make up your personal war zone. You have to get healed to be able to fully choose and fully experience identity in Christ. You have to get healed to choose victory and to make the move from victim to victor. You cannot allow your life to be driven by brokenness; otherwise, you risk being driven into all the wrong decisions, places, and things that take you away from God. At best, you become the double-minded man the Bible refers to in James: unstable in all you do. At worst, your entire identity gets derailed, causing you to live your life as a victim sharing your diseased mindset with those you love. For me personally, sparing my son emotional abuse because of my personal war zone was worth confronting my brokenness head on! To walk in the fullness of victory, every stronghold in your life has to be destroyed. Inner healing is the process by which this is achieved.

What exactly is brokenness?

Think of a plate—a fine piece of china or a nice daily plate. After some runs through the dishwasher, the plate gets some nicks and breaks on the edges. Then your kids bang the plate and drop it carelessly, a couple times, and there are more chips and breaks.

Over time, the plate isn't exactly the beautiful thing it was made to be when it came out of the box and into the world, but it still functions. It's fine for a lot of daily uses, where not a lot of people will necessarily see it. However, it's broken and chipped and not as nice as it was made to be.

Over time, you begin to realize that, sadly, the plate you once loved just cannot be used for all its intended purposes. When special company is over, you opt to use the new plate that isn't chipped and broken because you know it will make a more powerful impact when it's set on the banquet table for all to see. It's more effective and appealing for the job. Eventually, even your family and friends, who may have really liked the chipped and broken plate when you first bought it, begin to grab the new plate next to it. They naturally want to use one that's more attractive, and most likely, they've grown tired of getting scratched or cut by the original plate's rough, broken edges.

So it is with us as God's kids. The plate represents your heart—the emotional and deepest-feeling part of your soul.

Even with broken pieces and chips, we can function fairly well, day to day. However, those broken and chipped pieces of your heart, which are sitting there inside the cabinet, have names. Names like fear of rejection, sadness, depression, anger, anxiety—you name it. All of these make up the pieces of our heart that are broken off the larger plate of our lives.

Because of the scenario I described above, friendships are ruined, marriages are destroyed, jobs are lost, children are damaged, and lives are lived in complete despair. Victims abound because of brokenness based on everything that has occurred in our personal war zones.

Everyone wants to be the beautiful *desired* plate that functions perfectly in its role. Everyone wants to be the plate chosen to be set on the table for special occasions. Everyone wants to be new and unbroken. Everyone. I know I did.

When Roger gave me this cursory explanation of what brokenness is many years ago, I knew one thing for sure: I was broken. He knew, as did I, that I could not be married successfully without going through inner healing. I had to make a choice for victory in the area of marriage, no matter how much my brokenness screamed at me, *"Nooooo! You'll never be able to do this!"* Then I've had to learn to continue to choose daily to live in victory in my marriage and not resort to thinking like a victim—owed happiness by someone else and filled with a constant expectation of failure for a million reasons.

Much of how I reacted to things with my husband initially, as a partner, was driven by living with a victim's mentality and poverty of the mind. These were consequences of my brokenness. I fought him, I hid from him, I screamed at him, and I retreated into emotional fortresses my brokenness had created to protect me but that the enemy was using to destroy me. That's how it goes for anyone who is broken. The fortress that once protected you eventually hurts you and works to destroy you. There are no emotional places of escape that are truly safe.

Everything I have lived through and have had to overcome was, in fact, driven by the domino effect of the sexual abuse I experienced as a child and the resulting brokenness I carried with me. It weighed on me. It asked me daily to give up, to choose to be a victim, to let poverty of the mind set in and accept that I was born for nothing. My entire life—the low self-esteem, the pain, the sexual promiscuity, the drugs and alcohol I casually toyed with in college to numb the pain of heartbreak, the fear, the hopelessness, the anger, the inability to trust, and the ease with which I could shift out of one relationship into the next when the going got scary and tough—was all because of emotional brokenness.

That brokenness was rooted in events and traumas concerning not only my childhood sexual abuse but also my parents' divorce and my being raped as a teenager. Like many broken people, my life was full of things I could blame to remain living as a victim. Never fully understanding what was underlying the behavior that I knew was not me, my life spun out of control. You would have to read my first book to understand that my brokenness led me into an abusive first marriage, took me to jail in Italy, and drove me through fame and success like a vacuum cleaner, sucking up all the sin around me that my flesh desired. It also eventually exhausted me to a place of total surrender. In surrender, I finally came to the end of myself.

The end of yourself is the place you must be to choose victory that lasts! In this place, you know it's not about you and that you need help to walk in the victory you desire. In this place, you know that only God can do what nobody else can: heal you of your brokenness so you can live freely choosing to move from being a victim to being a victorious, overcoming man or woman on every level.

Many of you reading are at the end of yourself. In reaching that point, shout your choice for victory the loudest! That's right. Right now! If this is where you are, I want you to put the book down, jump up, and literally shout, "Thank you!" as loud as you can.

Why? Because this is where it no longer matters who or what is to blame. It doesn't matter whether the world is racist or not. It doesn't matter what handicap you have or what finances you lack. It doesn't even matter whether you can read these words! (That's what an audiobook is for.) When you come to the end of yourself, either God takes over and you *choose* victory or the enemy wins and you *choose* defeat—your reward for choosing to remain a victim.

As my husband explained the intricacies of brokenness, the way we act out because of it and the way the enemy will use it against us to keep us from our destiny by constantly destroying relationships and opportunity, I was floored to hear him describing exactly what my life, up to that moment, felt like. I was broken as a young girl, and my behavior, my choices, and my life mirrored brokenness as a young woman, no matter what success I achieved. No matter how attractive I was, I felt unattractive. No matter how loved I was, I felt unloved. No matter how many friends I had, I felt alone.

My brokenness was causing me to *choose* to think and act like a victim when life had given me victory.

Being understood brought a flood of peace to my spirit back then, and it still does today. I began to listen intently as a calm settled upon me. This was *it*. Roger explained how inner healing works and how it heals the brokenhearted because Jesus shows up supernaturally and binds up our broken hearts. Just then, I was suddenly filled with hope. If Jesus could heal me and set me free from the emotional captivity caused by my brokenness, I wanted it and I wanted it *now*. I wanted victory. I refused to be defined by the experiences that desired so strongly to define me as someone who should accept feelings of hopelessness and anger for what had been done to her. I refused to be defined by where I was born, how I was raised, and what happened to me growing up. I refused to be called a victim, by myself or anyone else. So I chose victory.

To know there is Someone who understands you, Someone who can fix it all, Someone who can set you free should be the greatest news you've *ever* heard. Yes, Jesus saved me in a prison cell in Italy many years ago, but this next level of saving would be the one that took me fully into my destiny. Only Jesus can heal you of your broken parts. You can be given tools to cope by a therapist or a faith that overcomes. I have tried both. My faith that overcomes is at work like a tidal wave, waiting to wash over my fears and give me the strength I need daily to continue to choose victory in Jesus Christ. Your destiny is waiting for you to make a choice. The *choice* is always yours.

Understanding brokenness and inner healing saved my life and completely transformed it into one in which choosing victory is the only option I am ever interested in. I am not interested in victim's narratives, victim's thinking, or victim's causes. I am *really* not interested in victim's parties and clubs. I *am* interested in solutions for victims to make the journey to victory because that is what God wants for your life. It's what He wants for your children's lives as well. It's certainly what He wants for our nation of broken people today.

Supernaturally, as I was healed of specific broken mindsets created by my childhood traumas, my son was healed of the same ones—or different ones that had formed in him because of mine. Why would my son be a concern, you may be thinking? Well, like many parents, he's what drove me. The exploding, moody, depressed, confused behavior that I saw coming from him at fourteen was terrifying to me, and I realized that my brokenness had actually, directly or indirectly, caused his. That's how it works with your kids.

Brokenness had formed in my son because broken people break others, as I've said before. But equally importantly, it formed because the sin I engaged in because of my brokenness had opened doorways, if you will, for demonic activity to come against not just me but against my child as well. That's what your *sin* does. When you have children and *you* walk in sin, you give Satan the keys to tamper with *their* lives. That's why you'll see generations of alcoholics, pedophiles, or rape victims. Drug users often have kids who use drugs or become sexually promiscuous. Sexual promiscuity and adultery by a parent can often lead to worse forms of promiscuity and sexual perversion in their children. These cycles are real and deeply spiritual. The only way they are conquered is by someone stepping to the plate with a deeper desire to gain the prerequisite spiritual knowledge of how to fight to win and to choose victory. (More on sin later!)

Now, understanding what brokenness and inner healing are, you may feel the need to shut these doors forever. That's great. I remember the feelings of urgency that made me plunge into my inner healing work like a student desperate to graduate in one semester. As I was healed, the work and the rights of the enemy to mess with me and with Christian were broken, one by one. As my broken heart was made whole, my son began to supernaturally change right before my eyes. Behaviors stopped immediately as I learned to take spiritual authority over him, my life, and my inheritances.

As my mind was transformed, I began to understand God's mind and heart. I began to see and think about things the way He sees and thinks about things. I began to realize that I had been brainwashed since birth by TV, magazines, music, and entertainment into some very incorrect ways of living, thinking, and viewing the world around and inside of me. These things told me I was right to feel like a victim by asking me to do and believe the things that victims do. Yet God sees me as a victor. If we can do all things through Christ who strengthens us, why on earth would we settle for anything less than full victory? This victory extends to our children, our friends, our communities, and our nation.

Needless to say, my work on myself completely changed my son. He has never been curious about drugs as I was. He has never been promiscuous as I was. He is grounded and thoughtful, not flighty and careless as I was. Brokenness and inner healing both affect everything and everyone around you, one way or another. As your mind and heart align with God's mind and heart for you, your children will begin to change because of your example. They will begin to align their thinking with that of someone who's a victor and not a victim.

The process of inner healing may take one session for some people and multiple sessions over a few years for others. I had some very complicated abuse issues, and for some reason, it is believed that highly creative people tend to break more, so my inner healing took longer. That's another book. Suffice to say that you have a very real enemy, and spiritually, he will wage an all-out war to keep you in captivity to certain mindsets.

If you're willing to do the work, however, God will never leave you nor forsake you. Every promise God makes in His Word is yours. When you get tired and weary just PUSH! Pray. Until. Something. Happens. And remember, as it says in Numbers 23:19,

God is not human, that he should lie, not a human being, that he should change his mind. Does he speak and then not act? Does he promise and not fulfill? (NIV).

One thing to remember in dealing with the heart and brokenness and inner healing: The world preaches, teaches, and lives in a self-indulgent fantasy by conditioning us to follow our hearts. I am going to make a statement that is completely countercultural, but with an understanding of brokenness and inner healing, I believe you will understand. How on earth do we follow our hearts when the Bible says, "The heart is deceitful above all things, and desperately sick; who can understand it?" (Jeremiah 17:9 ESV).

I never understood this scripture until I understood how brokenness and inner healing work. I was taught to follow my heart. I believed in the romance of the heart, and following it seemed like such a noble and victorious way to live. This is what the entire world thinks. For these reasons, this scripture never made sense. But when you understand brokenness and inner healing, you realize there is so much about your heart that is broken and misunderstood by even yourself that following it is *absurd*. I followed my heart into one victimizing relationship after the next with the wrong people. I made decisions driven by a heart that was broken, splintered, and operating at the childish age it was when I was first sexually abused. My heart lived as a victim, making choices that a victim makes. You cannot trust your heart. That is why you have a brain! Fight effectively against the unique facts of your personal war zone and use your God-given wisdom to make decisions. That is victory.

You may be experiencing—right now, even as you read this— that He is employing mercy and patience with you. There are things that have happened to you, experiences you carry with you, that only He really knows. That's why only He is fit to judge your heart. That's why I'm here to tell you to follow Him. Not your heart.

Your choice for victory lies in making the clear distinction between your heart and God right now. This will be hard for many of you. But, trust me, your heart is not God. God is not your heart. God is God. He knows truth. Your heart feels. Facts are not feelings. God heals the facts of your life that cause you to feel as the victim you may think you are today, turning you into the victor you will surely be tomorrow.

When your heart is made whole, you no longer have broken parts operating independently from the core of the plate. They no longer pop up irrationally to drive you into an emotion you don't want to be in. You are a whole, new plate, free of chips and broken pieces and able to be used for all the special occasions God created you to be used for. When you are healed of the broken pieces of your heart and the emotions running your life, everyone desires you. Everyone wants to be around you because they no longer get cut or scratched by your broken edges. You are safe to be around. And you are ready to shine on the banquet table of all your dreams and for all the purposes God has planned for your life.

Can you afford to go through life without this type of healing?

I say no because I tried it. Sometimes unknowingly, we all try it. No matter how hard we try to numb the pain, erase our realities, avoid thinking, lose ourselves in success and achievement, or distract ourselves with people and things, it's impossible to escape the reality that your life is out of whack when it's out of whack!

Even while running from God, most people know they aren't running toward a better substitute. You may think you are because your flesh feels good in a moment. But eventually, your flesh hurts and aches all over again. It's an unending cycle of up and down and high and low with brokenness. Getting the inner healing you need for your life enables you to no longer run but to live and receive victory.

That's why, for me, this is the greatest chapter in the book of my life thus far. Of all the lessons I have to share and all the messages I have to preach, nothing matters more to me than for you to understand that you are broken, and Jesus Christ came to heal you. Right now. Today. Victory is yours. And it's your choice! Your entire life depends on it.

FORGIVENESS

"Now my soul is deeply troubled. Should I pray, 'Father, save me from this hour'? But this is the very reason I came!" (John 12:27 NLT)

What is the very reason Jesus came? What is He referring to here? Forgiveness. The specific purpose of His life ... and the key that unlocks ours!

Just as brokenness encapsulates every facet of your personal war zone, forgiveness is critical to your foundation for healing and moving forward. Your personal war zone requires you to utilize the weapon of forgiveness more than any other.

I will begin by saying this about what's important to truly understand concerning forgiveness: God is too holy and righteous for us to stand before Him without dying. In fact, when He spoke to Moses, He said, *"You cannot see my face, for no one may see me and live"* (Exodus 33:20 NIV).

Because of our sin, we cannot stand before God and live.

Jesus Christ died for us so that our sins would be forgiven. He died so we would be considered righteous and *able* to stand before God without dying. Absent this free gift of love, you cannot fully see and experience the Father. In fact, many who haven't yet accepted Jesus describe feeling cut off from being able to pray or feel a wall exists between them and God. That wall always comes down the moment you encounter Jesus. You'll experience a great breaking free in your spirit the moment you turn to Him and acknowledge your need for God's forgiveness.

This puts into context the major reason for Jesus Christ. He came into the world to die for the *forgiveness* of our sins because our sin separates us from God and makes us unable to look upon Him. He is the sacrifice God chose so that we don't need to live separate from Him any longer. Because of Jesus, we are forgiven by God for the stuff that we do that surely needs to be forgiven. His whole gig was based on forgiveness. Why? Because we *all* need it! None of us could go before God without the supernatural cleansing this single act provided. Imagine standing in front of a magnificent fireball of light made of total purity. Imagine, with how dirty and ugly you can be sometimes, staring into that light. You would be burned up within seconds by the sheer force of good in comparison to your evil. We need a Savior because we need forgiveness. This is the single greatest act of love we embrace as Christians. Perhaps you get this and perhaps you don't. It doesn't matter because the principles of forgiveness are proven time after time as medicine for your own soul, not necessarily the souls of the forgiven.

How then can we hold anyone else in unforgiveness? We can't. To do so is to make a mockery of the entire example established in the very life of our Savior. To not forgive others is to bind your life to them—and worse, what they did to you—forever.

As generations continue to question Jesus and figure out who He really is, He continues to reveal truth. *"Thou sayest that I am a king. To this end was I born, and for this cause came I into the world, that I should bear witness unto the truth"* (John 18:37 KJV).

"For this cause came I into the world." What cause?

Why did Jesus, the Lord God Omnipotent who sits at the right hand of the Father, Creator of worlds without number, Lawgiver and Judge, condescend to come to Earth to be born in a manger, live out most of His mortal existence in obscurity, walk the dusty roads of Judea proclaiming a message which was violently opposed by many, and finally, betrayed by one of His closest associates, die between two sinners on Golgotha Hill? I wouldn't have. You wouldn't have. But He did. What was His cause?

His cause was love for all of God's children. Unique in His sinless perfection, He offered Himself as ransom for the sins of others. So that others, you and I included, would be forgiven.

We. Have. To. Forgive.

I had to forgive my parents for their divorce. I had to forgive my relative for sexually abusing me. I had to forgive the guys who raped me. I had to forgive people for lying to me, abusing my friendship, and being careless with my heart. I had to forgive colleagues and agents who dropped the ball on my life. But why? They were wrong. They didn't *deserve* my forgiveness. They deserved *punishment*.

The answer is simple. Because I, too, needed forgiveness. I too acted out, reacted, and lived in ways that were awful before God. I was too sinful to stand before Him without the covering and cleansing blood of Jesus Christ, which washed me white as snow. He whispered to me as He now whispers to you, *"Come now, let us settle the matter … Though your sins are like scarlet, they shall be as white as snow; though they are red as crimson, they shall be like wool"* (Isaiah 1:18 NIV).

We all need a bath. We all need washing from everything done to us, by ourselves and others. I did many things that didn't glorify our Father's beauty and my position as His daughter. Because of Him, however, we can believe that *"as far as the east is from the west, so far has he removed our transgressions from us"* (Psalm 103:12, NIV). This promise assures you that you now walk in the reality of your sins being removed. They've been removed so far that you can go to God in prayer, boldly asking for anything you know is within His will. What about asking Him to show you your brokenness, heal you of it, and give you the strength to forgive those who caused it to begin with? What if you ask Him to help you choose victory right now?

So you're only halfway convinced that you can forgive the awful people who have hurt you? You're not fully convinced you can forgive white people for having had slaves hundreds of years ago and rigging the system in their own favor? You're not convinced you want to share your good fortune with black and brown people who may not have worked as hard as you have? You're not convinced you are respected like the men are in business?

Well, let me explain what forgiveness is and what it isn't. Forgiveness doesn't mean that injustice doesn't exist or that the scales haven't been unfavorably tipped away from you. Forgiveness isn't a Disney movie! You don't have to live happily ever after with the pedophile who hurt your child. In fact, if my child was sexually or mentally harmed by someone, I would not hire that person to babysit my second child simply because I had forgiven him or her. Wisdom must be applied.

Let's take a deeper dive.

According to Wikipedia, forgiveness is the intentional and voluntary process by which a victim undergoes a change in feelings and attitude regarding an offense and lets go of negative emotions such as vengefulness, with an increased ability to wish the offender well.

In my words, forgiveness is giving up your right to judge. It's letting go of a person, event, or occurrence and giving that situation to God to judge.

Let's look at five categories of what forgiveness is *not*.
Forgiveness isn't ...

1. Condoning: failing to see the action as wrong and in need of forgiveness
2. Excusing: not holding the offender responsible for the action
3. Forgetting: removing awareness of the offense from your consciousness
4. Pardoning: granted by a representative of society such as a judge
5. Reconciliation: restoration of a relationship

Forgiveness won't have you stick around for more abuse. Forgiveness won't have you declare something isn't wrong when it is. Forgiveness doesn't dismiss liability; it dismisses judgment and refuses to hold on a moment longer to a harmful situation or person. Forgiveness unchains you from that person or event. Forgiveness releases a harm to God and trusts Him to correct all things, rebuke all things, punish all things, judge all things, and make all things right as He sees fit.

You will need to forgive, and in turn, you will need to be forgiven. Acknowledge all that you've done wrong in response to a person, event, or situation. By virtue of being broken by someone or something, you will have sinned in response. Usually the sin of anger is lurking inside you. Pray, and let the Holy Spirit bring to mind everything you need forgiveness for. When we think someone deserves our unforgiveness, we will surely have done things in response that will need to be forgiven as well.

After the Holy Spirit brings to mind the things you need forgiveness for, ask God to forgive you. Then prayerfully choose victory over every way that person or event has stolen your win and cast you in the role of victim and loser.

I was sinned against tremendously. But I sinned much in return. I was hurt and dropped and abused and betrayed. But I hurt others and dropped others and abused others and betrayed others. Jesus put it perfectly, *"I tell you, her sins—and they are many—have been forgiven, so she has shown me much love. But a person who is forgiven little shows only little love"* (Luke 7:47 NLT).

When you get real with yourself about how much you need to be forgiven every single day, you will fall more in love with Jesus than you've ever been. How can you not? Understanding how much He has forgiven me helps me understand how much I have to be grateful for. It helps you see how much of an actual victor you already are—and likely have been for quite some time. It turns you into the biggest advocate for victory for others through the sheer humility of realizing that you are just as bad as the next guy, really.

Forgiving those who've done you wrong, those who've mistreated you, and those whom you feel owe you something is the most freeing decision you can make in your choice for victory.

Why? Because life owes you nothing. People owe you nothing. Once you can accept this fact, then you can begin to move from victim to victor. Forgiveness allows gratitude to finally enter in and allow you to see the amount of thankfulness you should have for what life *has* given you and what people *have* done for you.

Unforgiveness toward others doesn't gain you anything positive. You don't gain freedom by holding onto unforgiveness. You don't gain insight by holding onto unforgiveness. You don't gain power. There is no restitution in unforgiveness. There is no redemption or movement forward. There is no victory.

What does come with unforgiveness is loss, lack, anger, and poverty of the mind as the currency of your spiritual bankruptcy. You will never win by holding onto your unforgiveness in your personal war zone. You will never achieve the life you want if you cannot forgive others and yourself and master the sin that makes up your spiritual war zone. Further, our nation will continue to be divided in the political war zone by individuals who are unable to forgive. Unforgiveness has numerous consequences that span generations and nations and continues into eternity.

Aren't you tired of being a victim of what was done to you? Forgiveness is the key that opens a very, very, big lock. I suggest you stop right now and quietly reflect on who and what you need to forgive before reading any further. Say out loud, "Father I forgive (insert name or event), and I give them to you to judge in Jesus's name." Once you say these words out loud, you will feel chains begin to break off of your life and your mind. Each chain broken will free you more and more to make your choice to move from victim to victor.

The life of Corrie ten Boom greatly inspires me. If anyone deserved to have the mindset of a victim, she did. Corrie and her sister were arrested by Nazis and spent several years in a labor camp before the Allies marched into Holland in May 1945. For more than three decades, Corrie traveled the world telling her story and sharing about God's forgiveness and the need for people to forgive those who had harmed them.

Corrie was put to the test in 1947 while speaking in a Munich church. At the close of the service, a balding man in a gray overcoat stepped forward to greet her. Corrie froze. She knew this man well; he'd been one of the most vicious guards at Ravensbrück, one who had mocked the female prisoners as they showered. "It came back with a rush," she wrote, "the huge room with its harsh overhead lights; the pathetic pile of dresses and shoes in the center of the floor; the shame of walking naked past this man."

And now he was pushing his hand out to shake hers and saying, "A fine message, Fraulein! How good it is to know that, as you say, all our sins are at the bottom of the sea!"

And I, who had spoken so glibly of forgiveness, fumbled in my pocketbook rather than take that hand. He would not remember me, of course. How could he remember one prisoner among those thousands of women? But I surely remembered him and the leather crop swinging from his belt. I was face-to-face with one of my captors, and my blood seemed to freeze.

"You mentioned Ravensbrück in your talk," he was saying. "I was a guard there. But since that time," he went on, "I have become a Christian. I know that God has forgiven me for the cruel things I did there, but I would like to hear it from your lips as well.

"Fraulein," he said again as his hand came out. "Will you forgive me?"

She wrestled with the most difficult thing she ever had to do. Corrie wrote, "The message that God forgives has a prior condition: that we forgive those who have injured us."

Standing there before the former S.S. man, Corrie remembered that forgiveness is an act of the will. It's not an emotion.

Jesus, help me! she prayed. *I can lift my hand. I can do that much. You supply the feeling.*

Corrie explains that, as she thrust out her hand, an incredible thing took place.

The current started in my shoulder, raced down my arm, sprang into our joined hands. And then this healing warmth seemed to flood my whole being, bringing tears to my eyes.

"I forgive you, brother!" I cried. "With all my heart." For a long moment we grasped each other's hands, the former guard and the former prisoner. I had never known God's love so intensely as I did then. But even so, I realized it was not my love. I had tried and did not have the power. It was the power of the Holy Spirit.

You may never hear the words "Please forgive me" from those who have inflicted injustice upon you. But at the end of the day, it's really not about them. Forgiveness is all about you.

PART II

The Spiritual War Zone

WHY DOES SIN EXIST?

The need to forgive wouldn't exist if we didn't have so many people making so many wrong choices. Absent wrong choices, one could expect that we would treat each other with love, honor, and kindness. God gives us free will because He loves us and desires us to *choose* Him, and His path, freely. Unfortunately, people use their free will to choose to do wrong things. Some of the consequences of these selfish choices can best be described by the words hate, confusion, disrespect, offense, and sin.

The spiritual war zone within each of us requires two critical things: a desire to fight and a willingness to change.

If you don't have a desire to fight against the wrong choices and desires in your life, you have effectively chosen to become their victim. Let me say that again so you understand the tremendous significance of it: *Your wrong choices will make you a victim and most likely victimize others.* No matter how good those choices feel. No matter how small they may seem. Your choice to do the *wrong* thing is your choice to *not* do the *right* thing.

Choosing to do the wrong thing—whether by choice, ignorance, or accident—is what the Bible calls missing the mark. For example, if a doctor cuts off the wrong leg in surgery, he has done the wrong thing. He has missed the mark. He may not have meant to, but tell that to the guy without his leg! In this case, the doctor would even admit that he made the wrong choice and missed the mark. Tragically.

The Bible's word for missing the mark is *sin*. Did the doctor sin against the man?

The word "sin" was a military/archery term for "missing the mark." An archer who shot his arrow and missed the target was called a "sinner." In war, missing the mark, being a sinner, could have grave consequences. People could die.

Think about this scripture: *"For all have sinned, and fall short of the glory of God"* (Romans 3:23, ASV). I know for a fact this one is true for me. When we make wrong choices, we miss the mark in life; we sin. If your aim is to do the wrong thing, then your aim is to sin. If your aim is to do the right thing but you mistakenly do the wrong thing, it is still sin.

Bad choices are usually the result of sin. Sin is designed to take you out. The wages of missing your mark are death, the Bible says.

I used to hear that verse and think, *Oh brother. That's absurd and extreme. Nobody is gonna die if I tell this lie or have sex with my boyfriend or cheat on him.* I really felt this scripture was a bit of proof that the Bible wasn't entirely real. How could death come on the heels of most people's normal behavior?

Then God began to show me this principle at work.

I went through a season of thinking I could do what I wanted with my body. Nobody would disagree that this is still the dominant thought in culture today. But every time I had sex with someone, I would lose a piece of jewelry—usually the nicest one I wore on my date. After about four times experiencing this, I realized that every time I had premarital sex I *lost* things. Always. Without fail.

Then I began to realize that it wasn't always a *literal* death that occurred when I missed the mark. But *something* died. It was *lost forever*. A friendship died. A relationship died. A job or an opportunity would die. Your reputation will die. *Something* will die in the wake of you missing the mark. That's how sin pays its wage: it makes you the victim of some kind of loss. Sin is the stuff victims are made of. In the long run, nobody really likes to be around sinners. They are filled with the fruits of their sin, and when you are seeking to live in victory, you can smell and feel their death all around you.

When you love someone who is continuously missing the mark in life, it's painful. I have come to a place where, absent God, I wouldn't be able to navigate what I am supposed to say or do when I realize that someone I care about has little desire to go to war against their sin. Some people need more guidance, mercy, and love because they may not even recognize the spiritual war they're in or the battle that needs to be fought. Others may be Christian, yet simply be in rebellion or unwilling to look deeper than the surface so as to avoid the reality of the fire they're playing with.

My least favorite are the Christians who justify their actions and personal desires by calling it "God." They are dangerous when God gives them a vision because, if they lack integrity or spiritual maturity, they often misuse and hurt others around them, calling it "God's will." They take and use, never being thoughtful or even concerned about the situations they put others in because they are so absorbed with the vision they think God has called them to.

People like this don't usually realize they are in the sin of pride, missing the mark constantly. Pride becomes their companion. It becomes so fortified they don't even notice the offenses they cause and the relationships they lose. Sadly, many leaders, because of their own pride, destroy relationships God may have brought them. It's no wonder the Bible says that *"pride goes before destruction, and a haughty spirit before a fall"* (Proverbs 16:18 ESV).

God would need to allow a fall to occur in order to stop the damage being done by the sin of pride. Damage to others. Damage, sometimes, to something He is trying to build. Damage even to the person who (most often unknowingly) is walking in pride. I believe God will allow a fall for protection—not only to protect the person, but to protect the many purposes that He may have for that person. Sadly, when you are the victim of someone's prideful behavior, you can get really hurt and offended. Offense, then, further perpetuates the sin cycle launched by the sin of pride. Pride creates a big ol' mess!

Let's stop a moment and look at pride. *Nothing will impede your choice for victory like the sin of pride!* The biggest thing God showed me is that pride is really deceptive. It's tricky and clever. Nobody wants to admit to being prideful because pride isn't godly, but often we just don't know when we are in it. God, who created everything, is not prideful. Pride, in fact, goes against the very character of God. Yet man desires promotion and elevation from his circumstances so much that pride can easily become his/her best friend.

Think about Jesus. God in the flesh. He became low, took insults, and was spit on and completely abused by people who were far less than He was.

So what does pride look like?

When you notice an attitude that says, "I got this, and I don't need anybody else's advice," you are possibly courting the sin of pride. That's not to say you should be running around seeking advice from everyone or feeling a lack of confidence in your abilities just to prove to yourself you're not in pride. But there is a bottom-line humility we sense in people who are intelligent and have a vision yet are still open to other people's opinions and advice. People like this live with sincere humility, recognizing they may not know everything.

Prideful people don't like being challenged and dislike criticism—both of which can usually be traced back to some sort of brokenness in the area of being put down or never encouraged as children. This will usually cause them to be dishonest and lie if need be to shield themselves from critique. Sadly, pride makes a person unwilling and unable to identify their own brokenness, so they are unable to be healed of it.

Pride is a sin that lies, cheats, steals, misrepresents, doesn't lead well, destroys visions and callings, loses friendships and relationships, and becomes consumed with self in a way that is maniacal. Yet God is so merciful; He is constantly rescuing people from their pride by stepping in front of the bullets being shot from the gun in the prideful person's own hands.

Pride will make you and your dreams victims of epic proportions. My friends, *do not despise godly instruction and wisdom*. Pride is a root of all kinds of sin, including the few I feel are worth mentioning here. It is an impediment to choosing victory in your life, even if you think you've made that choice and are walking in it.

Man's desire to be like God has been clear throughout history. It began in the Garden when Adam and Eve ate the apple. From the Romans to the Greeks to our hedonistic appetites for things that please our eyes and our flesh, we are groomed to partner with sin. And so much of it boils down to a desire to be our own god: pride.

Why does sin exist? Why do we miss the mark in the first place?

Sin exists because God loves us so much that He gives us free will. Let me explain the point I mentioned at the beginning of this chapter. If you were stranded on a deserted island with only one other person there to love, you would only have one choice. Therefore, the choice isn't truly free. It's a selection from the little you were offered. If, however, there were ten people there on the island with you, you would have a large field of people to choose from to love. In that environment, you are genuinely free to experience, question, and choose. The person you choose to love would be happy that you chose him or her from the large field of options you had.

This is how it is with God. He has placed us in a world filled with many things to choose from to satisfy our desires. Yet He longs for us to choose *Him*. When we choose to satisfy our desires outside of Him, we are often doing wrong and choosing to live with the consequences of sin.

The human heart is designed with many longings. Love, significance, beauty, intimacy, greatness, amusement, and to feel the love of God are the seven areas where I've noticed people seem to have the greatest desires for understanding and satisfaction. These are God-created longings; they reflect His own, as we are made in His image. There is nothing wrong in any of them—until we go outside of God to satisfy them. Sin is found in our going outside of God to satisfy longings that were created by God to be satisfied by Him. Deception and the multitude of wrongs our free will has to choose from creates our problems.

Sadly, many people choose to harm others. They choose to lie or steal. They choose to hate others based on skin color. Through things like pornography and sex trafficking, they choose to exalt male satisfaction over honoring women. Every day, year after year, man uses his free will to choose things that are wrong—seeking the satisfaction of human longings outside of God. Then they blame God for the consequences of the wrong they chose. In short, on the island of choices, they choose everything except to love God and live in the way He has prescribed for us.

Sin lies at the core of every disease we have, every problem we face, and every lie we believe. *Sin* has many faces, colors, attitudes, and economic positions. In fact, sin is the one thing we all have in common. There is no going from victim to victor without choosing first to get victory over sin in your life! The spiritual war zone is best summarized by 1 John 2:16: *for everything in the world—the lust of the flesh, the lust of the eyes, and the pride of life—comes not from the Father but from the world* (NIV).

In order to win in your spiritual war zone, you have to have a greater desire to do things consistent with godliness. This requires totally breaking free from pride. This is difficult in a world filled with broken people who don't all want to confront the personal brokenness in their personal war zones. People look for a million ways to compromise rather than make stands. They avoid rather than confront. It's easier to adopt the world's standards than God's. This leaves sin on the table as perfectly OK in our daily lives.

When doing the wrong thing is a perfectly acceptable part of your daily life, the attack on doing things in a manner consistent with what is right increases. In fact, if you look at the world we live in, you would be hard pressed to argue that the attack on doing what's right has been anything but relentless. Few make that choice, and even fewer are celebrated for doing so. Usually, doing the right thing is seen as weak and powerless.

So what is right and what is wrong? This is a good question because how you perceive what's right and wrong will affect how you see sin and what you consider sin to be.

When sin is as accepted, as it is in our culture, it's safe to say the choice for victory is one people feel they can make without choosing Jesus. The evidence of this is seen everywhere. Even when sin is classified as doing the wrong thing or choosing incorrectly, it reduces the definition of sin to humanly controlled behavior. In reality, sin without explaining the definition of righteousness as taught by Jesus suggests morality apart from Jesus. This is dangerous. We cannot allow sin to be relative; our plumb line has to come from the Word of God.

Yes, the Word gets manipulated by corrupt leaders when they have a sin problem. Jesus is seen as divisive and Christianity is laughed at because we have a sin problem. God has all but been thrown out of our systems, our schools, and our lives because we have a sin problem. Shall I say it plainly? You are a sinner because you desire to do wrong. Your inability to hit your mark is losing the war for our nation to be great.

Let's revisit Bethesda for a moment. Jesus heals the man, but the Bible doesn't say that He *only* healed him—He *made him whole.* God is actually interested in all-around wholeness. Jesus later runs into the man at the temple and gives him a very interesting instruction.

Afterward Jesus found him in the temple, and said to him, "See, you have been made well. Sin no more, lest a worse thing come upon you" (John 5:14 NKJV). Jesus takes time to make sure the man understands he was healed despite his sin issues but that, if he doesn't watch out, the sin issue could rise up again and make him sicker than before. We hate the idea of disease being the result of sin, but it is. People have taught on this subject with heavy condemnation and guilt, so even looking at it this way ruffles feathers. Maybe your feathers are ruffling right now! But we can't negate that Jesus warned the man firmly, *"Guard this wellness you have been given. Watch how you are thinking so that you don't fall into the old patterns that made you and kept you sick."*

Let me add to your understanding of all this. In Jesus's day, most cases of paralysis stemmed from sexually transmitted diseases.

I would be remiss not to propose to you that one of the sin issues this man carried was his incorrect thinking about how he saw life. He didn't look at himself as making the wrong choices and missing the mark he desired to hit. He didn't consider that he was a *sinner.* Instead, he saw all of life through the eyes of a *victim.* This gave no room for love, hope, or faith to operate fully in his life. It gave no room for victory. When we live as victims, we carry unbelief, which denies the possibility of our situation ever chang-ing. We lose hope and believe the lie that we have no more options.

Often, part of our healing process involves renouncing the sin of a *victim mindset*. We are not orphans. We are the sons and the daughters of God, and as Scripture tells us, all of creation groans and waits for us to be revealed. The orphan's mentality is the same as the victim's mentality. But you are not an orphan. You have a Father, and He has left you an inheritance. All He desires is that we choose faith, because as Hebrews says, *"without faith it is impossible to please God"* (Hebrews 11:6 NIV).

THREE DANGER ZONES

All of our inheritances are affected by our wrong choices. Sin is so deceptive and insidious that most people don't even realize they're in it. To make matters worse, the world we live in has disguised sin so well that wrong appears to be right, and right appears to be wrong. 1 John 2:16 tells us all sin comes from three tactical areas in the spiritual war zone that we must wage war in: *"the lust of the flesh, the lust of the eyes, and the pride of life"* (NIV).

Let's take a closer look at those three areas, starting with the lust of the flesh.

The Lust of the Flesh

I understood this area in my spiritual war zone to be extremely powerful when I read Romans 7:19, which says, *"For I do not do the good I want to do, but the evil I do not want to do—this I keep on doing"* (NIV). This hit me like a ton of bricks. I knew this reality on a deep level.

After I chose not to live as a victim, even though my life circumstances tried to define me as such, I noticed something. I wanted to live a certain way or think a certain way, yet I kept doing the opposite of what I wanted. Then I read, *"… if I do what I do not want to do, it is no longer I who do it, but it is sin living in me that does it"* (Romans 7:20 NIV). That sin for me was not just my rebellion or my sinful choices. It was the pain, anger, and fear inside me because of the sinful choices others inflicted upon me. Sin abounded. It was everywhere.

It was in my personal war zone. It was in my brokenness. It was in my sinful responses. Sin was everywhere. Sin, sadly, begets more sin. It envelopes many, if not all, victims from early on. I think of the beautiful faces of small starving children in Africa who are free of sin but clearly victims. Even in their situation, the sin of a world content to let extreme poverty and hunger exist is what causes their plight. Yet even they have the ability to choose victory and live free of sin, rewriting their victim's narrative, if they want to.

The *lust of the flesh* is real and powerful. It steals victory from us daily.

By now, you probably realize you are at war with yourself in the struggle to choose victory. If you read on in Romans, Paul writes, *"Oh wretched man that I am! who shall deliver me from this body of death?"* (Romans 7:24 KJV). Sin is at war with our flesh.

Our personal war zone makes us crave things we know are not good for us all the time. This lust creates the inner spiritual war zone we must fight in daily.

Let me elaborate. Your brokenness, created by the facts of your personal war zone, is used against you in your spiritual war zone to destroy you and any choice for victory you might ever attempt to make. No wonder Paul cries out, "Oh wretched man that I am!"

Imagine this scenario. You are struggling to deal with the emotions you have from being the victim of injustice. But the facts of your story—perhaps being born black and in a ghetto, with little food and even less hope—are at war with your ability to forgive. Therefore, your flesh lusts after things like money and what you believe you are owed. You have extreme entitlement and quite possibly anger. Because of all of this, even though you don't want to live this way because you know it's incorrect, you just can't walk in the truth that you know *is* correct.

This is the victim's cycle at work. Once victimized by others, now victimizing yourself. Yes, oh what wretched man, or woman, you might possibly be! To be caught in a life-and-death struggle between your flesh and your desire to move from victim to victor is tragic.

The Lust of the Eyes

The other thing we wage war against in the spiritual zone is the *lust of the eyes*. What are you looking at? What do you allow yourself to see? What is your soul eating because of what your eyes are seeing?

There are five gates into your soul. Your soul is your mind, emotions, and your will—what you choose to do. The five senses are the five gates. The eye gates allow entrance to many things.

You have heard it said that the eyes are the window of the soul. It's true. The eyes actually feed the soul in many ways. They take in many visions and images that seek to feed the desires of the flesh. In this age of visual stimulations and widespread pornography, we should be cautious. The soul can be scarred and the mind twisted in ways that can never be repaired simply because of what you might see and when you might see it. Children can be damaged in numerous ways by stumbling upon porn or other things they shouldn't see.

For an extreme example, consider serial killer Ted Bundy. The night before his execution, Bundy said his porn use started normally and then escalated, eventually getting to a point where he wanted to act out his fantasies.

"Like most other kinds of addiction," he said, "I would keep looking for more potent, more explicit, more graphic kinds of material. Like an addiction, you keep craving something which is harder, harder, something which gives you a greater sense of excitement, until you reach the point that pornography only goes so far."

He became addicted to regular nude pictures first. That progressed to images of sex. That progressed to snuff videos of women being killed while engaged in sex. That progressed to murdering women, which eventually landed Bundy in the electric chair. Many people experience traumatic childhoods, breakups, and porn addiction without becoming serial killers, but the progression of evil as linked to sin is undeniable.

Here's another example: My friend Lori, whose story impacted me deeply.

Lori's father loved taking family videos of her and her siblings, and as a five-year-old, one of her favorite things to do was to play them back later. She found such joy in those silly home movies.

One evening, in search of a moment of joy, she went searching for the tapes so she could watch one. She found one that wasn't labeled, so like any curious little child, she couldn't wait to find out what funny family moments this one contained.

When she put the video on, she didn't find a funny family moment. It was not her and her big sister and cousins being silly and singing songs or doing dance routines.

It was pornography.

She felt shocked, curious, awkward, and fearful as she watched the whole thing, unsure of what to do or think. In this moment, Lori says, it was as if something switched on for little Lori. From that day forward, she thought constantly and continuously about sex.

Eventually, the family moved from the house where she found the video tape into a home with a new offering: Select TV, which her father watched every night after she and her siblings were sent to bed. Lori explained to me that her dad didn't realize that every night as he was watching porn, his daughter was lying on the hallway floor, watching right along with him—for years. She began to fantasize about being a porn star. Sexual scenarios that she didn't realize were twisted and evil occupied her mind all day long.

Consequently, Lori could never focus in school. She never felt smart. Her self-esteem was extremely low. Her mind, as she describes it, was completely full of thoughts of the sexual images she fed on nightly all through her childhood—as if she had found something she could emulate successfully, as well as have her father's undivided attention. It's no wonder she grew up to have seven abortions, be raped twice, and deal with all manner of venereal diseases. Her life was on a fast track to mental destruction and death. She was a clear victim of so much sexual perversion and sin that it's unthinkable to imagine. Five-year-old little girls focus on dolls and playing games. They want to grow up to be princesses. They do not think all day about twisted and perverse sex and sexual abuse. They do not dream of themselves at five years old in those types of sick, twisted scenes. It's demonic.

And it was all a result of her father's decision not to guard his eye gate—an incredibly powerful doorway to life or death.

No matter where you are from or what circumstances you have endured in your personal war zone, your eyes are an important part of your choice to move from victim to victor. What you look at will affect your very soul. It will give you the strength to make the choice to live as a victor, or the proof you need to remain in victimization.

Matthew 6:22–23 tells us clearly how the eye gate affects us on a spiritual level: *"The eye is the lamp of the body. If your eyes are healthy, your whole body will be full of light. But if your eyes are unhealthy, your whole body will be full of darkness. If then the light within you is darkness, how great is that darkness!"* (NIV).

In your spiritual war zone, you'll gain great ground if you make a commitment to protect what you see and hear. What you allow through your eye gates will seep into your mind and eventually into your heart. Out of the overflow of the heart the mouth speaks. Be careful. If you claim to be a follower of Christ and want to love and honor Him, I would challenge you to really question the kinds of things you are allowing through the gates of your eyes. There has to be a fight for the eyes.

In Scripture, David says, *"I will not look with approval on anything that is vile"* (Psalm 101:3 NIV). David wanted to live a blameless life. To do that, he knew he needed to avoid temptations to sin, such as looking at wickedness. In a moment of boredom, David allows his eyes to gaze upon a naked, married woman: Bathsheba. Things are a mess from there. David watches Bathsheba bathing, setting off a chain of sin that ended with him lusting for her so badly he had her husband killed to get her for himself.

David was engaged in ancient pornography. His eyes were feasting on something he shouldn't have been seeing, and he was feeding his soul all manner of vile thought to go with it. Of course, Hell always feels like Heaven when you're walking in the front door, and Bathsheba was actually beautiful. But it was vile that David was looking at a naked woman. Especially a married one.

Pornography is a wicked thing. It really is poison. It is effectively destroying sexuality today and eliminating the purity of the kind of sex God created us for. In today's culture, we are literally surrounded by "vile things."

Ask yourself, "What am I allowing into my home?"

I think of some of the parenting mistakes I made because I wasn't more diligent about what I allowed my son to see on TV when he was a young kid. I remember meeting Dave Chappelle in Chicago. We were staying in the same hotel, and he was standing outside in the valet area smoking a cigarette one day. My son, Christian, who was playing basketball at the University of Kansas at the time, had been a huge Dave fan since he was a young boy.

In fact, I walked in the living room one day where he was laughing hysterically while watching his new favorite: *Chappelle's Show*. He was laughing so hard I wanted to join in the fun, so I lay on the couch next to him and started watching. It was a skit on STDs— and while it was very funny, especially before I surrendered my life to Christ, I was a bit uncomfortable with allowing my twelve-year-old to watch. It seemed a bit inappropriate. But, hey, all his friends were watching, so why would I say no?

I introduced myself to Dave in the valet area in front of the hotel that day, and much to my surprise, he recognized me from my work on TV. I was flattered. He was super kind and gracious. I explained that my son, now a college basketball player, and his friends were massive fans. I even asked if we could take a selfie together and record a little hello video on my phone for them because it would officially make me the coolest mom on the planet. He obliged.

After some time together, he stopped as if thinking something through. He said to me, "So, your kid is now in college?" I replied yes.

"Hold up. He must have been about eleven or twelve when my show was on. You let him watch my show?" he asked in a very parentally concerned manner.

I shifted, wondering if he was going to say what I already knew. "Are you *crazy*?" he asked. "I didn't even let my own kids watch my show!"

I smiled, embarrassed, and said the only thing I could. "Yes. I was *clearly* crazy." We laughed but the truth was the truth.

It may seem like an insurmountable task to parent your kids in this way, but you must. You are not charged with being their friend. They don't need to like you. They need to love and respect you, and that goal may cause them to be angry for a season. A season of you not being popular is worth their lives.

I started watching a new HBO show called *Euphoria* the week it premiered, and for the first time in my life, I was so shocked I turned it off ten minutes into the first episode. The show is nothing more than kiddie porn. Within the first few minutes, I had seen thirty-three images of a man's privates, all shown to a teenager. Whether it's an accurate presentation of what young teens are doing or not is irrelevant. It's a glorification of a major problem. The corruption of all the young people watching and involved in the series, and even more adults, with images of fourteen- and fifteen-year-olds engaged in sexual acts, is disgusting and wrong. It's the worst choice a creator or a TV network could choose to make. I've never seen anything so bad on TV, and it's sad that it's become the norm.

Whether we realize it or not, our hearts are affected by what we see. Don't allow the media to ruin your soul. Make war on the things that seek to annihilate you and keep you chained to victimization. You were created for victory, and choosing it is done step by step as you take control over sin, starting with your eyes.

The Pride of Life

We have looked at pride. But what exactly is the pride of life?

This phrase is only found once in the Bible, in 1 John. However, the concept of the pride of life, especially as it is linked with the "lust of the eyes" and the "lust of the flesh," appears in two more significant passages of Scripture concerning the temptation of Eve in the Garden and the temptation of Christ in the wilderness.

The pride of life can be defined as anything that is "of the world," meaning anything that leads to arrogance, ostentation, pride in self, presumption, and boasting. John makes it clear that the pride of life comes from a love of the world. It's hard to love the Father when you're in love with the world because its basic tenets have little to do with spirituality and living life with Christian principles.

The first time we see this temptation is in the Garden of Eden. Eve was tempted by the serpent to disobey God and eat the forbidden fruit of the tree of knowledge of good and evil. Eve perceived that the fruit was good for food, pleasing to the eye, and desirable for gaining wisdom (Genesis 3:6). She coveted the fruit in three ways.

First, it was appealing to her appetite. In short, it seemed that it would satisfy her "lust of the flesh." The lust of the flesh is about satisfying any of your physical needs.

The fruit was also pleasing to her eye. It was pretty. She liked the color. It looked good. The lust of the eye is about satisfying that which we see and desire to possess.

Finally, Eve somehow perceived that the fruit would make her wise, giving her a wisdom beyond her own. Part of Satan's lie was that eating the fruit would make her *like God, knowing good and evil"* (Genesis 3:5).

The pride of life is anything that exalts us above our station and offers the illusion of God-like qualities, wherein we boast in arrogance and worldly wisdom. Pride itself actually makes you want to be God. Eve wanted to be like God in her knowledge. She wasn't content to live in a perfect world under His perfect grace and care for her. This feels somehow like less for people with a pride issue. Pride makes you exalt your needs and desires above God's and above other people's.

Satan tried these same three temptations on Christ during His forty days in the wilderness in Matthew 4:1–11. He tempted Jesus with the lust of the flesh (bread for His hunger) and the lust of the eyes by showing him a vision of all the kingdoms of the world with their splendor. He tested him with the pride of life by daring Him to cast Himself from the roof of the Temple in order to prove He was the Messiah—an ostentatious display of power that was not in the will of God or His plan for the redemption of mankind. But Jesus, though He was "tempted in every way, just as we are," resisted the devil and used the Word of God to beat him.

Christians have always been, and always will be, lured by the same three temptations Eve and Jesus experienced. Satan doesn't change his methods. He doesn't have to because they continue to be successful. He tempts us with the lust of the flesh: sexual gratification, gluttony, excessive alcohol consumption, and drugs—both legal and illegal. He also tempts us with the "deeds of the flesh" about which Paul warned the Galatians when he told them that *"sexual immorality, impurity, sensuality, idolatry, sorcery, enmity, strife, jealousy, fits of anger, rivalries, dissensions, divisions, envy, drunkenness, orgies, and things like these"* would disqualify them from entering the Kingdom of Heaven (Galatians 5:19–21 ESV).

The enemy tempts us with the lust of the eyes, as evidenced by our endless accumulation of "stuff" to show we are successful and victorious. We fill our homes and garages and have an insatiable desire for more, better, and newer possessions. All of this serves to ensnare us and harden our hearts to the things of God, so much that we measure victory in terms of external things rather than internal.

But perhaps our enemy's most evil temptation is the pride of life. Why? Because that is the very sin that resulted in Satan's expulsion from Heaven. Satan desired to be like God, not to be a servant of God (Isaiah 14:12–15). Likewise, the world doesn't measure victory by choosing to serve God but by how much you are able to serve your flesh.

The arrogant boasting that constitutes the pride of life motivates the other two lusts as it seeks to elevate itself above all others and fulfill all personal desires. It is the root cause of strife in families, churches, and nations. It exalts the self in direct contradiction to others. It exalts the self in direct contradiction to Jesus's statement that those who would follow Him should take up their cross and deny themselves. The pride of life stands in our way if we truly seek to be servants of God. If we don't serve God, we will serve ourselves. If we serve ourselves, we will be snared by sin. The focus on a self-serving lifestyle leaves room for greed and envy and all manner of hatred toward your fellow man. It is the arrogance that separates us from others and limits our effectiveness in the Kingdom. The pride of life "comes not from the Father, but from the world." And, as such, it is passing away with the world. Those who resist and overcome the temptation of the pride of life do the will of God, and "the man who does the will of God lives forever." This is true victory.

Choosing victory is all about choosing to defeat pride, lust, and anything else that exalts itself against the knowledge of God. There is no way to shake the victim mentality that may have grown in your personal war zone if you can't find any reason to live for anything more than your own desires. Without a greater vision, you'll find yourself severely unable to fight effectively against sin in your spiritual war zone.

MONEY, POWER, FAME, AND SEX

The love of money is a sin that easily trips up all victims. Sadly, when you've been denied having enough, it's easy to make money a main priority. Once you do, the lust for it can consume you for all the wrong reasons. Conversely, when you have plenty of money and having more becomes your main focus, greed will steal your life—leaving you with tons of things, yet nothing that is real or lasting. Many close friends of mine have sacrificed lives filled with the true victory of family and friends for the trappings of wealth. That only serves as evidence of their poverty of the mind.

Contrary to popular belief, money is not the root of all evil. The *love* of it is. The love of it becomes the lust for it, and that is where the slide into sin escalates. We fall victim to the fortified illusion of what money provides—but the illusion is entirely deceptive. Scripture says, *"And some people, craving money, have wandered from the true faith and pierced themselves with many sorrows"* (1 Timothy 6:10 NLT).

The assumption is that money is power and power is money. However, the weakest men I have ever known had plenty of money. They wanted victory, yet never conquered the battles they needed to win in their personal and spiritual war zones. This left them as empty vessels disconnected from true feelings and a true love of humanity. Material wealth and external victory, without any real personal or spiritual victory over the inner man, is the worst kind to have. For truly, what does it profit a man to gain the whole world but suffer the loss of his own soul, his marriage, his kids, his inner peace, or lasting love?

Power

Power is as deceptive as the love of money. Sadly, people with power are not always powerful people. People who seek power are often bullies who have chosen to remain victims because they refuse to do the work to heal their pain. They have enough to victimize others in an attempt to make themselves feel better. Yet they never feel better about themselves no matter what they do or who they bully. Their sin is rooted in pain, fear, and low self-esteem stemming from brokenness in the personal war zone.

Seeking power over others is a sin wrapped up in the exaltation of self, pride, dominion, and a lack of faith. Power is about creating victims, yet it is equally about remaining a victim yourself! Choosing to walk in victory requires a choice to abolish your need for power and accept humility and servanthood.

We define "spiritual power" as faith in a higher power, a consciousness, offering a sense of peace, contentment, confidence, and hope. When you are connected with this limitless, loving energy, you feel good, positive, and relaxed. Worldly power always comes with a component of fear and anxiety. Once you have achieved power in the world, have you ever noticed that fear and anxiety over how you'll keep it tend to creep in?

Our world has a dominant assumption today about the nature of power. Power is seen as good if it "accomplishes" the sorts of things you believe in but bad if it doesn't—or worse, if it "accomplishes" things that go *against* your belief system.

Many Christians have come to believe that the ends really do justify the means, even when the means themselves are evil. I see this in how they do business all the time. The question of power penetrates every sphere of human existence and, sadly, shows up in the mission and activity of the church.

Most young people desire to be culture-shapers. They even have a title for it in the pervasive voice of social media—"influencers." The title feeds the craving to be a leader, to feel relevant, to impact culture.

Many of the Millennials I see strive to achieve a seriously warped amount of power without an understanding of life, history, and people. I think about the young girl who called herself a vegan activist, rescuing sixteen rabbits while causing 100 baby rabbits of the rescued mothers to die, and I get sick to my stomach at her lack of understanding of what it means to be an activist. Yet as she posted on social media about her escapades, she received applause for her superficial explanation of what really occurred. In reality, she traumatized hundreds of rabbits and caused many to die. This fake power only emboldens her to do more harm in the pursuit of more power for herself and her cause.

Sadly, I see misplaced grandiosity driving many spiritual leaders around the world—a worldly view of power in leaders thinking they can wield it for Kingdom ends. Trying to do this only warps the core of their message, and more profoundly, I see a warping of their souls. Worse still, they are warping generations of young people into believing there is something more majestic about temporal power than spiritual power.

At the heart of the biblical view of power is Paul explaining that God's power is made perfect in our weakness!

If we contrast a worldly vision of power with a Christian one, we see the world believes power is attained in our strength for the sake of control and typically domination, whereas a Kingdom vision of power is that it is received in our weakness for the sake of love. Kingdom power is received, not taken. This is why Paul says, *"Therefore I will boast all the more gladly of my weaknesses, so that the power of Christ may rest upon me"* (2 Corinthians 12:9 BSB). Paul's power in the Kingdom comes from lack and weakness because he relies on the power of Christ. Paul doesn't see himself as powerless, needing to grab power in his flesh. He sees himself as all powerful because he receives the power of God in his weaknesses.

People living with a victim's mentality rarely see their weaknesses as strengths because they often build multiple walls that keep them from choosing Jesus, much less victory.

True Kingdom power is power in weakness. Therefore weakness is not something to be destroyed, avoided, or ignored. It is something to be embraced. Yet this runs contrary to the prevailing assumptions both outside and within the church today.

So we learn to wield our strengths at our problems, thinking that God is really calling us to be savvy enough, strong enough, and sophisticated enough to make a difference. This confronts us with the question Paul asks in Galatians 3:3: *"After beginning by means of the Spirit, are you now trying to finish by means of the flesh?"* (NIV).

I think many of us assume choosing victory in situations is about choosing which skill you have and using it successfully. But in reality, choosing victory is about submitting your problems to God and waiting for Him to act in concert with you as you do what He says.

Not enough people, leaders or otherwise, are reflecting upon the implications of all of this. We cannot seek to advance the Kingdom and the Gospel in the flesh rather than in the Spirit. We cannot employ a vision of power for good in a way that undermines the Kingdom value of the work. And we can no longer teach in such a way that the *"cross of Christ be emptied of its power"* (1 Corinthians 1:17 NIV).

The Christian choice is, in fact, a life of power. But it is not the power of our flesh, nor is it the power on sale in the world. The power of God we are called to embody is known only in our weakness. You have to ask yourself, with all your visions and desires for the future, in all of the various careers you may be called into, does your vision for power align with Jesus's call and Paul's articulation of what this looks like? Or have you bought into the assumption that, if you do something with enough savvy and sophistication, your actions will be unblemished by the power you employ?

Your answer to those questions will determine much of how open you are to Jesus's proclamation of the Kingdom and how willing you are to have faith in Jesus and live life His way.

Power lies in renouncing sin. That largely lies in renouncing yourself and your own fleshly desires to live outside the tenets of God's Word. It's not easy, because many of us have embraced lies that go to the very core of our being. For example, there was a time when I believed with all my being that kids and marriage were not for me. No way. No how. Then out of nowhere, a craving for children came. To this day, I have yet to identify where this desire came from. But if you ask anyone who knows me, they would define me as a complete mom and extreme lover of children. My son is my life. Our spiritual sons and daughters mean the world to me. Being part of them, and them being part of me, is the joy of my life. Yet before seeing the sinful attitudes behind my reasons for not wanting kids, I wasn't interested.

It's the same with marriage. I never believed I could be truly committed. My issues had issues and my walls had walls. There was so much brokenness, so many reasons and excuses for why I couldn't really commit, that I ruined more than one potentially great marriage proposal.

Fame

If an attachment to money is greed, then an attachment to fame is part and parcel of the pride of life.

I remember the first big stadium show my "brother," Lenny Kravitz, played at Bercy Stadium in Paris. I was floored looking out over thousands and thousands of people, all screaming and crying and worshipping … my *brother*. My friend from high school, Lenny was always a rock star to me. But to see years of dreams happening before my very eyes was mind-blowing. He was a *rock star*. On the stage, I could feel the energy. It was powerful. It was spiritual. His fame was godlike. Suddenly, I was overcome with the thought that this could become really hard for him, or anybody in his position. How on earth could someone *not* become twisted by the idolatry involved in this kind of fame?

After the show, in his dressing room, I asked him, "Honey, how on earth will you keep *this* in perspective?" He looked at me seriously and said, "Girl, it's hard." Amidst the lights flashing and the people clamoring for autographs, we shared a somber and mutual acknowledgement of the fact that humans were not created to be gods. Nothing about fans, fame, or the idolatry people make of flesh is divine.

Fame tries to elevate us into a place were only God should sit. If you allow yourself to enjoy that place, pride will surely blossom. Pride always seeks equal footing with God. It seeks adoration and honor. It is the antithesis of God, and it always goes before a fall because we are not God, nor are we gods.

In the spiritual war zone, I feel safe in saying that never before has such a sinful idolatry captured people in the way the lust for fame has today. It is so strong that fame itself is enough. It doesn't need to include talent, wealth, skill, or power; just fame. Evidencing a serious need to be recognized, loved, liked, and seen, we are at a crisis point in trying to satisfy our longings for significance outside of God.

Sadly, the deceptive lusts we feed will never satisfy our souls. Sin is designed to consume and be consumed. When you try to feed your soul something you cannot consume enough of, something that will only consume your soul in return, you begin to understand the danger zone your spiritual war represents. Sin never builds up or gives back. It only steals. In any belief system or culture where sin abounds, there is no lack of victimization.

You've heard the phrase "fame is fleeting." That's because by its very nature, it is constantly changing. If happiness were to be found in fame and fortune, wouldn't the world's richest and most famous people be the happiest on earth? Trust me, they are not. The most famous people I know seem to enjoy the limelight for a season, but then it quickly becomes a burden that robs them of the ability to live a simple, ordinary life. One day, they may be famous and adored. The next, they may be forgotten. One day, they may be rich. The next, they could lose it all.

The pursuit of fame is a victim's body oil. You rub it on to feel better about yourself, and eventually your own success becomes your undoing. Eventually, you will arrive at the point where your fame has been tolerated long enough and the world turns on you. One only needs to remember the child stars who were once so loved before the media turned on them and devoured them to see the truth of this. That which you consumed now consumes you.

I think about my own struggles with the minimal amount of fame I've experienced, and I remember how hard it was to walk away for a season and move to Kansas to be nothing more than a wife and a mom. While these roles have been the most gratifying of my life, I grew up craving a career. Fame for me was part of the payback I would give to life for mistreating me. It was the big finger to everyone who ever abused me or dished out injustices upon me. It was a need for revenge—and to surrender that, in all honesty, is one of the hardest things I've ever done. Many victims want revenge. I wanted to prove to the world that I was worth more than the way I had been treated.

Being a woman and a person of color always presents much to overcome. Worse is that you can actually *feel* when people don't believe you can get where you want to go. You can sense the smirk in their heart. I believed success was the best revenge. I remember experiencing physical withdrawals from the need to attend every event I was invited to and to keep in contact with people who really weren't friends—as if my identity was defined by my fame, the doors it opened, and the amenities I enjoyed. Breaking through to the other side of needing anyone's validation, invitation, or affirmation is the greatest victory I have ever enjoyed.

Fame is nothing to be desired. It is not victory. It is applause, and it is often applause for no reason at all.

Sexual Immorality

The ultimate weapon of mass destruction in our society today is that of sexual immorality. It is the oldest sin of rebellion that we return to constantly as people. It's also the greatest destroyer of the individual spirit. It causes chaos, confusion, and division even inside one's self. The epic presence of sexual immorality in our society today is rooted in an absolute loss of personal and spiritual identity. There is no victory to be had until we choose to confront the victimization we allow to flourish in this form. From our TV shows to our bedrooms, we call what's wrong right and what's right wrong. If your goal is to move from being a victim to being a victor, it's critical you stop and consider how sexual immorality serves to victimize you over and over again.

I was conditioned by the environment I grew up in not to wait for marriage to have sex. In fact, an old girlfriend, Candace Bushnell, wrote a book called *Sex and the City* that became a hugely successful TV show. It defined an era of sex and dating for millions of young women, myself included. In hindsight, I laugh all the time at the fact that the show was run by gay men. In effect, my entire attitude toward marriage, sex, and dating was influenced by gay men and friends who were not looking for monogamous relationships. I identified with them! This is not a knock on anyone, but there is a major problem when a normal Sunday Christian girl realizes her entire world is inadvertently being directed by either gay men or straight commitmentphobes. I wanted sex without marriage, so a life influenced by shows like *Sex and the City* actually worked for me.

In all honesty, I saw myself as a victim, and in order to stop being one, I had to be in control. That meant controlling men, controlling my career, controlling my emotions. If I was in control, that was victory for me. I was attempting to do in my flesh what only God could do in the spirit.

Bottom line: I had a sin problem I wasn't interested in confronting head on. I had an inability, and sometimes a flat-out refusal, to fight in my spiritual war zone against the sin I was ensnared in because I had never really confronted the facts of my personal war zone. My brokenness from the things that happened to me as a young girl had created mindsets and fortresses that were rooted in sin. Anger against God and people caused rebellion. Lack of understanding robbed me of the ability to fight to win.

Even if you're not a born-again, Spirit-filled Christian, I know you'll get this the same way I did when a girlfriend of mine said to me one day that she had implemented a six-week rule in dating.

"A six-week rule?" I replied, confused. "What is that?"

She went on to explain that if she had waited six weeks to sleep with any guy she had ever been with, she wouldn't have had sex with 99 percent of her exes.

Hindsight being 20/20, I realized neither would I, for the most part. It dawned on me that she lived more in line with the Bible than I did, and she was right. It also made me realize that maybe the Bible I professed to believe in was right also. Celibacy was not something I had yet embraced, so I had sex when and if I felt a connection with someone. (I just hate that word. "Connection." It's so ... so ... deceiving!)

In accepting that I had actually jumped the gun in nearly all my relationships, I opened my eyes to a huge reality. Not one of the guys I had been with would I have chosen as a husband. Thinking I was the one with power, I usually ended each situation but was left feeling as if some piece of me had been taken. Worse, I felt unloved and unwanted in any real way because I kept choosing men who weren't loving me or wanting me in a real way. They got the cart before the horse and, through my own fault or theirs, never got to know the horse at all. I finally came to the conclusion that If I waited to have sex until I was married, I might actually save tons of wasted energy on guys who were not worth it and find a husband who was. Fornication as a sin, for me, just didn't work. There was no victory in it. With every walk of shame home the morning after, there was only the little girl victimized all over again—this time by her own choice. *Sex and the City* never explained this part honestly at all!

A sin problem requires a choice most of us simply don't want to make and often don't know how to make. Perhaps because sin feels good or because you are lazy or because you don't understand the true consequences of sin, you refuse to fight. Perhaps it's just the reality that nobody else around you is fighting against sin. The question still remains: Will you fight sin in your spiritual war zone, or will you lay down your weapons and go along with the status quo?

Whatever it includes or however long it lasts, your season of sin equals a choice to remain a victim, and that choice doesn't carry power. Your choice for sin is a choice against victory. But Jesus is always there to save, to help, and to lead. The choice for Him holds certain victory. Ever the gentleman, however, He leaves that choice to you.

I am going to go biblical and explain some things. Oddly enough, the word most often translated in the New Testament as "sexual immorality" is *porneia*. This word is also translated as "whoredom," "fornication," and "idolatry." It means "a surrendering of sexual purity," and it primarily refers to premarital sexual relations.

From this Greek word we get the English word *pornography*, stemming from the concept of "selling off." Sexual immorality is the "selling off" of sexual purity, and involves any type of sexual expression outside the boundaries of a biblically defined marriage relationship.

It may seem wrong to connect sexual immorality and idolatry, but they most assuredly are. Consider 1 Corinthians 6:18, which says, *"Flee from sexual immorality. All other sins a person commits are outside the body, but whoever sins sexually, sins against their own body"* (NIV).

As believers, we see our bodies as "temples of the Holy Spirit" (1 Corinthians 6:19 NIV). Pagan idol worship often involved perverse and immoral sexual acts performed in the temple of a false god. When we use our physical bodies for immoral purposes, we are imitating pagan worship by profaning God's holy temple with acts that He calls detestable.

Biblical prohibitions against sexual immorality are often coupled with warnings against impurity. The word "impurity" in the Greek is *akatharsia*. *Akatharsia* means "defiled, foul, ceremonially unfit." It connotes actions that render a person unfit to enter God's presence. Those who persist in unrepentant immorality and impurity cannot come into the presence of God. Jesus said, *"Blessed are the pure in heart for they shall see God"* (Matthew 5:8 NIV, cf.

Psalm 24:3–4). It is impossible to maintain a healthy intimacy with God when our bodies and souls are given over to impurities of any kind.

Sexuality is God's design. He alone can define the parameters for its use. Biblically, sex was created to be enjoyed between one man and one woman who are in a covenant of marriage until one of them dies (Matthew 19:6). Sexuality is His sacred wedding gift to human beings. Any expression of it outside those parameters constitutes abuse of God's gift. Abuse is the use of people or things in ways they were not designed to be used. The Bible calls this sin. Adultery, premarital sex, and pornography are all outside God's design, which makes them sin.

The following are some things I commonly hear as objections to God's commands against sexual immorality:

It's not wrong if we love each other. The Bible makes no distinction between "loving" and "unloving" sexual relations—only between married and unmarried people. Sex within marriage is blessed (Genesis 1:28). Sex outside of marriage is "fornication" or "sexual immorality" (1 Corinthians 7:2–5). But how can it be logical to do something that inevitably hurts you and argue that it was done in love or not in love? If it hurts, it hurts. When you give your body away to someone who doesn't stick around for the entire life journey, it hurts. Period. Whether you loved each other or not. We should expect commitment and honor and all of the love that is meant to go with sex. When you sleep with someone, you become one with them. Yes—one. All that they are becomes all that you are.

I love the next argument. *Times have changed! What was wrong in biblical times is no longer considered sin.* Choosing victory involves principles that never change. Most of the passages condemning sexual immorality also include evils such as greed, lust, stealing, etc. I find it funny that, in the war zone of spiritual sin, we have no problem calling these other things sin. Yet in terms of sexual immorality, times have changed, and God is somehow now wrong? God's character does not change with culture's opinion. If God is God at all, then to think He is as wishy-washy as we are is a huge insult.

We're married in God's eyes. This argument implies that God is cross-eyed. The fallacy of this idea is that the God who created marriage in the first place would retract His own command to accommodate what He has called sin. This is ludicrous. God declared marriage to be one man and one woman united for life (Mark 10:6–9). The Bible often uses the metaphor of covenant marriage to teach deep spiritual truth about our relationship as the Bride of Christ. To undo this one is to undo the entire foundation of our choice to receive salvation in Jesus. God takes marriage very seriously, and His "eyes" see immorality for what it is, regardless of how cleverly we have redefined it. I can never be so vain or stupid as to think I can pull one over on God!

I can still have a good relationship with God because He understands. I understand how easy it is to try to walk the line of sin by applying the love and mercy of God as a blanket covering. Grace is an incredible thing. We live under grace. Yet I am really weary of hyper-grace teachers and teachings that have completely diluted the need for repentance and turning from sin. Proverbs 28:9 says, *"If one turns away his ear from hearing the law, even his prayer is an abomination"* (ESV). We fool ourselves when we think we can stubbornly choose sin and God does not care.

This makes me think about a recent season of ABC's *The Bachelorette*. The series caught the eye of a lot of Christian viewers because there was an openly vocal, loud, proud, Southern belle beauty of a believer on! It seemed like hope in a bottle for Christians who, like me, thought we were going to be represented well on the show by seeing some lifestyle choices for victory on display. It got even better when she seemed to be in love at first sight with a Christian boy named Luke (my favorite apostle). This was off to a good start for me.

As the season progressed, I watched in shock and horror as our sweet Christian girl behaved proudly and loudly about Jesus while essentially bragging about her sin also. In fact, when confronted by the Christian boy because he had normal reservations about being with a girl who was willfully nailing a bunch of guys, she became enraged and led the societal mockery of him, his faith, and the actual truth of the Word of God that she proclaimed to believe. If there was a spiritual war zone to fight in, she chose to fight any Christian who made her feel guilty for wanting sex with a bunch of guys she had no intentions of marrying rather than fight her desire for sexual sin. The entire country of unbelievers, and many believers, celebrated her as fierce and powerful and a role model for their daughters. *Whaaaat?*

I watched with knowledge of one thing: She would end up more alone than when she arrived at the *Bachelor* mansion. She would end up alone and sad, crying in a room so nobody could see the pain, when she realized she was the loser. It was obvious that she was being set up for a huge attack by an enemy she did not understand, yet she was decisively courting rebellion.

I was right. She is currently alone. I dare say, as adorable as she is, and as much as my heart hurts for her, she brought about her own public humiliation. She is a broken baby Christian. When Satan is done with her, I pray she finds her way out of the victimization she chose for herself to a choice for victory as rooted in Jesus. A real choice for Jesus involves a real love for Him. As He said, *"If you love me you will keep my commands."* You'll at least try.

I don't think any of us reach perfection or total righteousness as Christians. But at some point, we have to stop playing games with the Word of God and own the rightness and wrongness of our choices. We have to stop trying to dress up the consequences of our sin.

God's expectations for His kids are crystal clear. *"Let marriage be held in honor among all, and let the marriage bed be undefiled, for*

God will judge the sexually immoral and adulterous" (Hebrews 13:4 ESV). Sexual immorality is wrong. The blood of Jesus can cleanse us from every type of impurity when we repent and receive His forgiveness. But that cleansing means we *try* to put our old sinful nature, which includes sexual immorality, to death. The best way to walk in sexual purity is to understand His word and be clear about how much He actually loves you.

SPIRITUAL WARFARE AND THE ARMOR OF GOD

Choosing victory over sin involves recognizing what the enemy is using against you personally and the weapons we each possess to fight back!

Finally, my brethren, be strong in the Lord and in the power of His might. Put on the whole armor of God, that you may be able to stand against the wiles of the devil. For we do not wrestle against flesh and blood, but against principalities, against powers, against the rulers of the darkness of this age, against spiritual hosts of wickedness in the heavenly places. Therefore take up the whole armor of God, that you may be able to withstand in the evil day, and having done all, to stand.

Stand therefore, having girded your waist with truth, having put on the breastplate of righteousness, and having shod your feet with the preparation of the gospel of peace; above all, taking the shield of faith with which you will be able to quench all the fiery darts of the wicked one. And take the helmet of salvation, and the sword of the Spirit, which is the word of God; praying always with all prayer and supplication in the Spirit, being watchful to this end with all perseverance and supplication for all the saints (Ephesians 6:10–18 NKJV).

When I read this scripture for the first time with real understanding after nearly thirty years of living as a victim to sin, I was overwhelmed by a depth of clarity and purpose. Suddenly, the wisdom of God settled upon me, and I realized: the state of mankind's existence here on earth is one of spiritual warfare.

This is why I say the spiritual war zone is the most critical. Whether you believe in my Jesus or not, you must recognize that your fight is not with people but with powers and principalities that *use* people to steal your life and deny you victory at every turn. If you can do this, then perhaps you'll realize how much you need my Jesus.

God's enemy hates all that is godly—including His children. He wages war against our very lives to stop us from ever walking in the power of knowing and living for God. God's Word is truly a lamp unto our feet, and as we follow it, we go from victory to victory in Spirit and in truth. This terrifies the enemy of our souls.

My own personal war zone included a fight that was never against humans. It wasn't against my half-brother who sexually abused me. It wasn't against the two young men who raped me at fifteen. It wasn't even against those who, in my mind, lied to me, abandoned me, abused me, or used me. My war all along had been against the enemy who uses sin in people as a weapon to make victims of others.

Evil is real. It's palpable, and you can feel it. It takes many forms. Jealousy, strife, terror, and confusion are all the fruits of evil.

You may often feel these things in people, in situations, or in events. These are good indicators you need to take your war to the spiritual realm. Our spiritual enemy uses our weaknesses and fears against us and others. Only through standing in faith, with the knowledge of how to put him in his place, do we prevail.

In my experience, even we Christians don't like to discuss Satan and spiritual warfare. It's scary to some and uncomfortable to others. Acknowledging the existence of a spiritual enemy who is pure evil, who holds court in this world, and who wants to destroy us constantly is kooky stuff. He is the opposite of our Heavenly Father. Yet his existence is very real. If God is faith, Satan is fear and unbelief. If God is victory, Satan is the all-time victimizer.

I believe God has allowed me to understand spiritual warfare on a deep level through my personal experiences. He constantly uses me to help others identify it in their own lives. The teaching He does through me comes with an anointing of purpose and revelation that far outweighs my intellect.

God is the God of victory, not of victimization. He is the God who enables us to choose to shed the victim's narrative of our lives and embrace the vision of victory He truly wants for us.

How?

By understanding how to put on the armor of God described in Ephesians! This is how we win in our spiritual war zone. We have a very clear and simple set of instructions for victory so that the lies the enemy has used since the beginning of time will not triumph over us.

We wrestle with demonic attacks of all sorts. Words, for example, are a simple illustration of how victimization passes through generations. Parents often speak life-defining projections over their own kids, not realizing they are crippling them or creating a narrative for their lives. *Hey, kid, you are stupid. You're not smart. Your sister is beautiful, but you aren't. We are poor. You won't ever be able to afford that.* There is life and death in the power of the tongue.

The things you say matter. Victory speaks victoriously. Not that I am suggesting you hide your head in the sand and pretend life is great when it may not be. But the choice for victory requires you to see many more angles to the puzzle of your escape from your circumstances than you often do.

We are taught in the Bible that our fight is not against these people. It is against the evil in their words. It is against the damage done to our souls by the things people say and do, often unknowingly. We have to be able to climb out from under the victimizing weight of all the statements made against us.

We also need to be able to climb out from under the weight of the ugliness we may have seen day after day, year after year. Images are powerful. Images of poverty, broken-down buildings, graffiti, filth, downtrodden people, all contribute to a powerful victim's narrative. Imagine the bleakness of a child's life when the sun is overshadowed by a drab, gray existence. Some kids grow up seeing green grass and trees and other kids laughing in parks. Others grow up in concrete jungles, seeing rats and garbage and faces filled with despair. Living and thinking like a victim is more likely for those with the latter experience. The soul fed a steady diet of victimizing images and narratives has a tremendous weight to break free from in order to choose victory. This is a fact. But as difficult as it may be, consider the alternative.

This is why I love traveling, especially for young people. Allowing yourself to see more than your neighborhood is usually critical to understanding that there is more for your life you can hope for out there.

The Armor of God

Back to battling! We win by putting on our armor daily. As a Roman soldier prepares for war, Paul explains that dressing our spirit and mind in the armor of God defeats that pull from deep inside to accept the victim's narrative written for you.

... Therefore take up the whole armor of God, that you may be able to withstand in the evil day ...

There is a full regimen necessary to choose victory daily. We are not told to put on one piece of armor. We are told to put on the full armor. A soldier wearing only ankle shields may not get pierced in his ankles but could get pierced through his chest when the attack begins. Your enemy knows where the weak, uncovered places are. Your openings are visible to your enemy when you are at war. He knows how to win. You better know how also or you'll lose.

So many people choose to remain victims because they leave themselves uncovered in some way. Don't be someone who blames God for the things you could have done better or the things someone else did. Victims blame. Victors accept responsibility and continue arming themselves.

... and having done all, to stand. Stand therefore, having girded your waist with truth ...

After you've done everything to arm yourself with the knowledge and wisdom He provides in His Word, stand and wait in faith. God did not give you incorrect or bad instructions, so put on your armor, take the field of battle, and wait for your enemy, knowing you're fully equipped to win.

At times, you'll still find yourself feeling like a victim—but you will learn to recognize the things that make you start to drift that direction. The truth of God's Word is that you are *not* a victim, no matter what has happened to you in your life. You are, according to the Word of God, very much a victor. You can do all things through Christ. You are the first and not the last. You are everything the Word of God says you are. The choice, as with any truth, is yours to believe or not.

... having put on the breastplate of righteousness ...

Our righteousness is only found in Christ Jesus. It's why, after trying everything, I chose Him as my Savior. Without Him, none are righteous. He died for us to be seen as righteous before God. Accepting Him covers our heart like a breastplate covers the heart of a Roman soldier.

The first thing to break in an attack is our heart. Righteousness, however, heals your heart and protects it. An arrow through the heart kills. It kills dreams. It kills visions. It kills hope. Hope deferred makes the heart grow sick, the Bible tells us. This piece of armor is essential because, as we live life and experience things that break our hearts daily, there is a great temptation to become bitter, angry, or depressed. Life is hard for many. But more than anything, it's that the heart becomes hard in response to life.

A choice that involves Jesus is a choice for the righteousness we have in Him that guards our hearts, enabling them to be filled with love.

Can you choose victory without faith? Yes. But faith in Jesus wins the war for victory when victimization wages a war in your spirit, mind, and body. He is a Savior who cares. A Savior who promises victory. Why would you not choose Him?

… and having shod your feet with the preparation of the gospel of peace …

Having repented, you are prepared everywhere you go to share the gospel of peace. Once you've chosen not to live as a victim, helping others find victory is easy and essential. It's essential because you'll realize that sharing peace requires you to constantly feed on words that bring peace. Constantly feeding on truth is required to keep the personal war zone from continuously rising up in your spiritual war zone to convince you that you really are a victim.

When you begin to win at spiritual warfare, you will start to bring words of peace into every room you enter, dismantling much of the warfare you might otherwise encounter. People today are so filled with tension, anxiety, and anger. They have questions about so many things. And they have many incorrect replies that seem to make sense when they are desperate for answers.

This is why the lack of knowledge of the Word that runs rampant in the church today sickens my stomach. We are at war, with zero depth of understanding of how to fight it. Instead, we focus outwardly, fighting people. We live like immature, ill-equipped representatives of a powerless, confused God. Victory calls us to realize that we carry a truth that works if we don't compromise it.

... above all, taking the shield of faith, with which you will be able to quench all the fiery darts of the wicked one ...

Every Roman soldier used his shield to deflect arrows from striking him. Our faith is our shield. I will say again, without faith, it is impossible to please God, so picking up your shield of faith pleases Him. Faith displayed in action, against every attack that tells you day after day you are a victim, is faith that eventually wins the war. Our faith may weaken in a battle, or even be non-existent in one battle versus the next, but our faith will eventually reveal, even to us, our victory.

The wicked one will attack you. God isn't hiding the ball. Life isn't a rose garden. It has thorns and worms in it. But even a rose was given thorns to protect itself, and we have been given armor, if we choose to wear it. Faith is *the* critical piece of our armor. Picking up your shield of faith every time that victim mentality begins to pull you down is your greatest weapon!

... And take the helmet of salvation ...

I love this one. There is something beautiful in realizing that my very belief in Jesus and what is promised me in salvation protects my mind daily. When you ride bikes, skateboards, or motorcycles regularly, you know a lot about needing to wear a helmet. If you fall, you want something there to protect your head from banging on the ground. Brain damage is a horrible thing.

Your mind is where most of your battles take place. Anyone who chooses to wage war in the zones of life that I discuss in this book understands that the mind is a weapon under constant attack. I call it a weapon because it's also where you win, when you understand spiritual warfare and the significance of the helmet of salvation.

That said, I've come to understand how fragile even the believing mind, much less the unbelieving one, really is. It is a fertile place, where thoughts and ideas, good and bad, can take root and grow into all kinds of things great and small. Diseases or cures, blessings or curses, all take root in the mind.

All sin begins in the mind as a thought, feeling, or idea. In your personal war zone, when you ponder the inequity of your life, your mind becomes a nurturing ground for all kinds of feelings—pain, anger, fear, disappointments.

Unbelief grows in the mind as well. I think unbelief is the greatest force that attempts to penetrate our helmets because our faith pleases God, enables us to walk in victory, and is the prerequisite to the helmet of salvation we are given. Unbelief can spread like a cancer through your mind and eventually throughout your entire life. It permeates cultures and nations.

The helmet of your salvation is a hard hat around your head. It serves to keep out confusing doctrines and lies against the truth of your choice to move from victim to victor. Knowing to whom you belong and what you believe will protect your mind from an onslaught of life's continual attacks.

... and the sword of the Spirit, which is the word of God ...

As a soldier, a sword is the weapon you use to mortally pierce your enemy. The sword of our spirit is the actual Word of God given to us directly by Him. The more we know of it, the more effectively we can use it to destroy the attacks and works of our enemy against us. "My people are destroyed for lack of knowledge," God says (Hosea 4:6 KJV). When we choose not to know God, we choose to perish. I am amazed constantly at how many people claim to be Christians who don't really read or study the Bible. They have zero knowledge of what they say they believe. Because of this lack of sincere relationship, we slowly die on the vine of life, becoming more and more comfortable with living as victims without any understanding of the fact that we were created for victory.

Think about how loudly the thoughts and words in your mind scream at you that you're a loser and can never be a winner. This inner dialogue is the one that is the most concerning within our spiritual war zones because it's a war with the voices inside our own mind.

At the height of my own realizations about this, I had earned millions of dollars and achieved great success. I lived in an incredible home across the street from Brad Pitt and Jennifer Aniston. I should have heard different voices. But the voices of victimization rage just as loudly when success is present. Anyone who has ever battled with himself or herself in this way will immediately understand the level of spiritual maturity, knowledge, and commitment it takes to emerge victoriously. You must be spiritually mature enough to go to the place you find victory. You must know where that place is. You must commit yourself to applying the knowledge once you gain it. This is how you emerge victoriously.

The Word of God itself is our sword. And not just His Word, His *rhema* word. That means His word spoken out loud. Let me explain.

There was a time I used to walk through my home saying Scripture out loud until an attack on my spirit, which was waging itself inside my mind, ceased to be effective. I didn't even realize then I was engaging a piece of my armor. I was using His *rhema* word to fight. It worked every single time. If I felt fear, I spoke Scripture about God not giving me a spirit of fear but of power, love, and a sound mind. If I felt tempted to have sex with someone I was in love with but not married to, I spoke out loud that if I would resist the enemy, he had to flee from me. I employed my sword, and I went to war on the feelings and impulses I wanted to act on that I knew were sinful and self-destructive.

I didn't even know back then, in the year 2000, how much power there is in the spoken Word of God. I only knew that when I used it out loud against feelings that had made me a victim to behavior I didn't want in my life, I won. God would deliver me to victory because I *chose* victory.

The only way to fight feelings is by using your sword. The only way to fight even people around you who offer you comfort in being a victim, as if something is owed you, is by using your sword. The only way to fight the unbelief that plagues all of us who say we have faith is by using our sword and by going to war against the constant attacks the enemy deploys against us. Spiritual warfare is real. Choose victory and use your sword.

… praying always with all prayer and supplication in the Spirit, being watchful to this end with all perseverance and supplication for all the saints …

So much can be said for this simple directive. Praying always. For all people. Ask yourself this: Do I care enough to pray always for anything, or anyone, besides myself?

In our selfish, entitled Millennial age, I dare say the levels of vanity and selfishness that my generation ushered in are now on steroids. People can't even see how self-consumed they are. I see a generation of twenty-somethings actually self-absorbed enough to think they're the only ones asking the questions they're asking, making the mistakes they're making, and experiencing the messes they're experiencing. Even the age-old journey of questioning God's existence seems to be something many feel is exclusive to them and their heightened intellectual existence. It would be hilarious if it weren't so vainly tragic.

We are challenged here to understand that continual prayer for others is part of the spiritual war zone because the converse is true in the world. The enemy of our soul desires for us to see only ourselves, our own pain and suffering. He desires to have us pray continually for the things we want, never thinking about the needs of others. This total self-absorption, even in our prayer life, has kept many people in a myopic cycle of seeing only their own victimization, unable to see that others too, feel pain.

Prayer is the most powerful weapon of redemption, recovery, and reason. It redeems what you feel you have lost. It recovers your ability to love all people, even those who have spitefully used and abused you, and it provides reason where none exists.

The enemy is winning on many levels, however, because of the sheer vanity in the world today. We feed young people a diet of milk and sugar, wanting God to be easy and palatable and never wanting them to feel threatened or challenged or uncomfortable because, after all, that's no fun.

Since when did we lose sight of the fact that everything about being spiritually mature, and ultimately successful in any battle, is about feeling uncomfortable and challenged? When did any Roman soldier ever feel comfortable and unchallenged on the field of battle? War is about death, people. The sooner you wake up and realize that your life, your kids' lives, and your family's lives are at stake, the sooner you can get to the business of obtaining victory in the war against you found in prayer.

Remember, only one war zone is about you—and this isn't it.

One of the main functions we have in serving each other and functioning at our highest and most effective is in prayer for each other. I spent five years of my life as an intercessor. I prayed daily for every child on my son's basketball team at the University of Kansas. I prayed for his coaches, whom I sometimes hated because many of their coaching tactics went against every single thing I know to be true about love and mentorship, not to mention good parenting. I prayed for the other parents—the ones I loved and the ones I found impossible to even like. I prayed for the university, the town, and the entire state. I sat for hours a day and prayed. In that state of having my heart submitted to loving and seeing them all as God did, He poured much revelation and understanding into me.

He gave me the ability to love and value others as He does and to forgive and pray for their growth and spiritual maturity. He taught me to care enough to pray for all the saints—even the ones who often resemble sinners. The things that were rooted out of my heart in this season of constant prayer opened my eyes to the shocking reality of my own need for constant prayer and forgiveness too.

Our victory, plain and simple, in the spiritual warfare we live in here on earth is found in prayer. We must pray for each other. We must pray for protection and covering from the various forms of spiritual warfare and attacks we all endure around the world daily. Our highest power as the body of Christ is not about any single person but about every single person standing in prayer for the next. That is a choice for victory.

In his writings, Paul tells us he is not making the enemy more important than he is but that we should simply not be ignorant of our enemy's ways. Understanding that spiritual warfare is real was part of my choice to move from victim to victor. It was part of my choice not to believe the victim's narrative over my life but to believe the victorious proclamations over why I was created. Most importantly, it was part of my choice to forgive others.

Spiritual warfare explains everything you need to know about the truth of good and evil. It explains how we win by not becoming like the evil around us and, possibly, like the evil done to us. It explains how a person can know that he or she is having their spirit repeatedly attacked and assaulted by people, feelings, and things, both seen and unseen. Spiritual warfare illustrates how God can have a beautiful plan for your life. So beautiful that your very existence creates fear and hatred in the heart of Satan. So much that he will dispatch a team of demonic activity at you to thwart Gods plans for you, like nothing your worst human enemy could ever achieve on their own!

We wrestle not against flesh and blood but against powers and principalities that use humans unwittingly, even those who love you, to poke into your deepest wounds and fears. This is to cause you to stop, give up, leave God, and go any direction but the one He has created you, prepared you, and equipped you to go! God is *not* to blame for your pain, your doubt, or your confusion. He is *not* telling you that you're worthless, that your efforts are stupid, or that you should abandon your hopes and dreams. He is *not* telling you that you are doomed to live as a victim, with a victim's reward of unhappiness and dissatisfaction. Satan uses his warfare, waged in actions, events, and words through others, to accomplish his goal of stealing your calling, stealing your hope, stealing your joy, and ideally stealing your life and your identity. He wants the victory you have been promised in Christ in exchange for the loss he was handed at the cross.

I Forgive Myself

We have already discussed the general concept of forgiveness in the personal war zone. Forgiveness in the spiritual war zone involves forgiving others of what they have done to you, but it also includes forgiving *yourself* for the sins and mistakes you've made in response.

The biggest limitation on choosing to walk in victory is when you *realize* how much you *deserve* judgement for how badly you've victimized others. Forgiving ourselves is a huge next step in choosing to move from victim to victor. This is difficult without confronting your own shame and guilt—the additional legacies of sin.

As with forgiving others, you need to understand that you have sin in your life. You are not innocent. You've done wrong. We all have. You don't deserve forgiveness. You deserve punishment. You deserve the wage of sin.

But you are loved, and forgiveness is yours if you repent and choose it. Refusing to forgive yourself means that Jesus somehow didn't do His job in dying to wash you free of your sin. *He is faithful and just to forgive us our sin, and to cleanse us from all unrighteousness* (1 John 1:9 KJV). That is His promise to us who choose to believe that He is who He says He is. That includes you.

PART III

The Political War Zone

POLITICAL BROKENNESS

Proverbs 14:34 tells us, *"Righteousness exalts a nation, but sin is a reproach to any people"* (ESV).

Today we are experiencing a cultural civil war! It is unlike any civil war we have ever faced as a nation because inherent in it is destruction and control like never before. It is more than divisive. It is deceptive. It's not about Democrat or Republican. It's about Good versus Evil, with Evil often disguised as Good. This war zone is about national control of the human spirit, the destruction of mankind, and completely banishing God as a matter of law.

Is that inevitable? Does the law of the land really matter? Does the makeup of the Supreme Court ultimately achieve or destroy

God's will for all of us? Can you legislate righteousness? How should we as Judeo-Christians live and represent our beliefs today?

God gave us very clear examples of how to govern well. The Bible provides a mountain of information about politics, government, and we His people.

Sadly, however, when I look at my country, at best I see a lack of identity. At worst, I see the wrong identity—that of victim rather than victor. This lack of identity is about brokenness, sin, rebellion, and an unwillingness to surrender. At the core of our confusion, anger, and fighting, we have lost our national sense of what it means to be America. This is tragic. I never thought I would be ridiculed for loving my country, but I have been. Sadly, this ridicule came from many people who have never traveled to another country to gain insight into why they should love America so much.

Millions of people in our world today are broken. They come from circumstances that have been less than ideal and from people who were likely broken themselves. As a nation, we live in a political war zone because we refuse to fight against the wrong inside ourselves.

Sin is often (not always) why we get broken in the first place. While we will discuss this at length later, suffice it to say that people harming each other and living far below accepted standards of morality will always equal a nation in turmoil. When the individual people who make up a nation accept evil as part of their life equation, there cannot be unity. When individuals live in rebellion against basic human decency, there cannot be political peace or national pride. When citizens are unwilling to surrender to a higher authority, there will only be broken people bumping into each other with their anger and unmet expectations.

Broken people hurting and harming each other is what I see as America today. We have settled for being victims while victimizing others in return. Victims do not listen to each other. Victims do not care for each other. Victims expect to be compensated by others while living in a continual state of anger and entitlement. Victims are incapable of understanding each other and don't even attempt dialogue. There cannot be victory as a nation when a victim's narrative is driving it. There can only be broken and angry pieces of a whole. There can only be what resembles war. When there is war on the inside, the political war zone creates political brokenness, which only serves to create and nurture political victims.

I see a country made up of people whose dreams are bigger than their circumstances, and for that, they feel stuck in Hell. On good days, this reality is almost too much to bear. On bad days, the anger at others is so thick it exists on its own. When your dreams are bigger than what you see around you, the warfare inside you and through you will often destroy you and everyone around you.

What exactly is political brokenness? How do we mend it in our nation?

Political brokenness is the sum of all our personal and spiritual brokenness! When we do not fight in our personal war zones and when we are lazy and uninterested in fighting in our spiritual war zones, we cannot help but become a nation that is completely broken politically. Our political war zone requires every individual to desire victory over their personal circumstances, their sin, and their brokenness. The only effective weapon in this war zone is that each individual is committed to his or her personal fight. A choice for victory in the two more personal war zones is required for victory in the third zone that affects us all.

We are in a tremendous war to emerge from the political brokenness we are all feeling and experiencing today. Yet it won't be a specific candidate or political party that heals our political brokenness—it will be a collective grassroots effort. It takes victors, not victims, to heal a nation, because only victors are interested in healing.

When a group of people are broken, a nation cannot be anything else. Because we are politically broken, we are suffocating on what society calls political correctness. Political brokenness offers us victims' groups in the place of God and political correctness in the place of truth.

Our desire to love and accept everyone, mixed with our political and spiritual brokenness, has concocted a powerful and deceptive cocktail called the *PC Culture*. As a nation, we are completely drunk from it. Worse still, we have offered it to the world, which will face an even worse hangover than we will.

Dressing Up the Lie as Truth

What exactly is political correctness? It goes a little bit like this:

"Mommy, the Emperor is naked!"

"Shhh, darling. Don't tell him. We will look very uncool and not at all 'hip' or 'loving' or 'accepting' if we say that!"

"Yes, but Mommy, that doesn't change the fact that he *is* naked."

We can stifle discussion about it—whatever *it* is. Dress it up. Dress it down. Give it an award at the Oscars and a Grammy for best new artist. That still doesn't change the fact that we are being forced to accept lies as truth. Wrong is still wrong, and sin is still sin … no matter what you call it!

Who is influencing whom? A nation influenced by lies cannot ever experience victory. When you recreate your past, you run the risk of repeating it. When you glorify your past, you run the risk of overlooking things you should grow from and not repeat. When you are a nation influenced by sin while choosing to turn a blind eye to the truth, your end is certain. We can interpret truth correctly or incorrectly, but never is the actual truth subjective. What you think of the truth may be different than what I think of the truth, but never is the truth the variant; we are. Choosing victory involves choosing to look at facts. If the emperor is naked, then he or she is naked. Now what?

A victorious nation must begin by nurturing victorious citizens. By that, I mean you have to desire that every citizen lives from a victorious narrative. One of the ways to do that is to stop prioritizing entire victim groups and classes of people as if they have no recourse in life. When I look at a small child who has no food and lives on the street, I am going to feel awful about what I see. But if my immediate heart reaction is to put him in a victim's box, label him as part of a victimized group, and shower him with pity while feeding him a steady diet of victimizing narratives, I have limited him tremendously. He will have to play out the limited choices that exist in the group scenario I've put him in. He adapts that limited group dialogue and lives with the limited hopes and dreams he feels exist for *his* group. In this way, as a nation, we have effectively nurtured a victim.

If my heart goes out to this young boy but my immediate heart reaction focuses on how to help him choose to live from a mindset of victory, he may overcome his limited external circumstances rather than succumb to them. If we feed him a victor's narrative of hard work, hope, and the stuff champions are made of, I assure you that, having raised plenty of young boys, he will grow up to change the patterns of whatever class of victims you would have limited him to with your misguided empathy. He will grow up filled with belief in himself, and that belief will carry him much farther than your pity will. A nation that abolishes victim's narratives and entitlements and focuses on providing hope for all its citizens is a better nation. This is a nation making a choice for victory for itself and all its people groups.

Who are victorious citizens? Any who choose to be. When the mindset of the various individuals and groups that make up a nation becomes one of contribution and not entitlement and victimization, we will begin to heal from our political brokenness. When forgiveness is a reality in the heart of every citizen, we will begin to move forward into individual and collective victories on a grander scale than most can imagine.

Political brokenness is aided by forcing us into a culture of political correctness at the expense of freedom of thought and speech. The PC culture that has plagued our nation involves accepting lies on nearly every level. We have made a complete victim of the truth. In fact, the truth is simply inconvenient when it doesn't fit the PC narrative created for *"thought victims."*

The PC culture kills original thought. It kills free speech. It kills religious freedom. In our political war zone, I believe that political correctness is another avenue for Hitler-like control of citizens, thinking them lesser human beings. I may not like what you have to say about me, but I support your right to say it. Because my right to express my view about you is freely supported, I must in turn support the same for you.

The fear of this freedom is rooted in the fact that we know people choose to do wrong with their freedoms. They choose to hate and harm rather than to love and edify. They choose to say things we deem politically incorrect. Yet denying someone's ability to express himself because what he says isn't politically "correct" is to deny the truth of what's in people's hearts to surface. Good or bad, right or wrong, it is only the truth that sets us all free. There is wisdom and understanding found when the truth in a person's heart is allowed to surface, no matter how ugly. But political correctness has no interest in the truth—only in the control that denying you the comfort to speak freely provides.

Political correctness is all about control. It is not about love, nor is it even about respect for others. Dishonorable or disrespectful systems will find a way to exist. I prefer to know the truth about my enemy rather than the lie of my friend. Governments that hide truth do so to maintain control of people. When information, thought, and freedom are stifled, it is to manipulate the direction of people's lives—your life. A PC culture is dangerous. Everyone in it is subject to being labeled something they are not merely because they ask a question or dare to question a system of thinking.

I will go so far as to say white people are victimized in a PC culture and minorities are suppressed. White people dare not say a word about programs created for minorities, question whether it is unfair for whites to be denied, or feel that they are overlooked without being labeled racists. On the other hand, when minorities are fed a lifelong victim's narrative, it only serves to either create toxic entitlements or destroy tremendous potential by disguising the labeling of them as less than whites. Nobody wins in this scenario.

When our emotions are manipulated by the PC culture we have accepted as protecting and loving people, we are in fact only ignoring others.

For the most part, we are a nation that wants to be loving and kind to other people. We have opened our hearts, minds, and borders since our inception (although a great rabbi once said to me, "Be careful not to be so open-minded your brains fall out your head"). We have become so open-minded that our brains are doing just that. We are being asked to do things without order. This can only create chaos and anger. Look at us. By classifying people as victims, in need of help at any cost, we have in effect victimized ourselves at great cost.

Why? Because our understanding of what love really is is completely wrong. Love contains order, in that it is patient and kind. It doesn't keep a record of wrongs. It rejoices in the truth.

Again, that word: truth. Political correctness does not rejoice in, delight in, or celebrate truth. It suppresses it, attacks it, and condemns it as unloving. When truth becomes our victim, we have stopped loving.

Our misunderstanding of love begins with our misunderstanding of God as the embodiment of love.

Our Love versus God's Love

God's love is unconditional. It is honest. It celebrates and delights in truth. It is patient. It is kind. It is longsuffering. It doesn't keep a record of wrongs. That means it forgets the things that have occurred in the past and moves forward with kindness, patience, and truth into the future. A nation built upon God's love is a nation that is not politically broken but a nation that has chosen to walk forward in victory.

Our attempt to create a politically correct society is damning us all to Hell by silencing the truth of what we see and know is wrong. Worse still, it is silencing any dialogue about what is right, wrong, or even truthful. We are dumbing down generations of young people as we allow them to be deceived into thinking that love means never telling someone the truth!

The truth of our current culture of deception and acceptance of all things, disguised as progressiveness, is just laziness coupled with an underlying lack of love. We are deceived by our notion that love is accepting of anything and everything people throw out there as true and desirable for them.

In reality, really loving people takes hard work. It means really getting involved with them and their messes. It means listening to their interpretation of truth for them, seeking to understand, and often to help heal or guide them. I often say that love is spelled T-I-M-E. Time is something none of us like to give without gaining something we want in return. That is not love. It is self-serving. The truth is that it is much easier to just sit by and idly watch people do what they want to do. Who cares?

However, this lack of concern for your fellow man is a choice against victory for all of us as a nation. Why? Because what you may feel unable to speak about, or desire not to get involved with, has likely already involved you. Directly or indirectly, our individual choices have a ripple effect on other citizens. When what you want to do infringes on how my children grow up or how I choose to live my life, my not caring about you and your choices has to be confronted. My lack of loving you or caring about you is now impacting society. While even my laziness would dictate that I stay over here in my lane and you stay in yours, our lanes will eventually collide. Then what?

Then I have to *care*. Because our PC culture may have stifled me into a place of not caring, speaking up, or confronting you, when you have driven into my lane and my rights are infringed upon, we have a problem.

This is where we are. We will always drive into each other's lanes because we share the roads. This is where every nation finds itself. Loving its citizens is a huge job for a nation. But that job begins in the hearts of individuals. The choice to love yourself must become the choice to love others, which becomes the choice to love our nation.

If I may go here for a moment, America can never be great until she begins to deal in truth. God's truth. Not your truth or my truth or their truth or our truth but God's truth. I will go even further to say that the only God whose truth includes loving all of us is the Christian God. If you study some, you will find that, while every other religion involves the people preparing a banquet table of food and good deeds for their god, the Christian God prepares a banquet table for His children. We serve a loving God who loved us first. He desires only that we fall in love with Him.

Falling in love with Him means you will fall in love with His view of love. Love isn't silent. Love doesn't sit idly by while you stay in your lane and I stay in mine. Love rebukes and criticizes and guides. Think about raising your kids, if you have any. You wouldn't allow your child to just do whatever he or she pleases. You would care enough to get involved. You will get messy when they make a mess. You will try to stop them from making mistakes, and you will put them on time-out when they do wrong. For the most part, there is no laziness in parenting when you love your kids. It is unnatural not to care what your children do.

Societies that place political correctness above the truth of God's love are societies that are lazy and do not care about their citizens. They are societies that have exalted the rule of flesh above the rule of God and morality. They deem self-satisfaction greater than service. These societies eventually fall because they have forgotten, or perhaps never accepted, that *righteousness exalts a nation, but sin is a reproach to any people!*

Is there room for this kind of messy, time-consuming love politically anymore? To elevate the nation to victory on the political battlefield, we have to *make* room for that kind of love, or we will never fully move forward from the victim's mentality that plagues us as a nation.

God's love looks very different than our love. We have to accept and understand this. And, more importantly, we have to model it in how we deal with the many conflicting demands, ideas, and opinions that shout loudly at us from every angle. *What would Jesus do?* This is truly the question we should be asking daily. What would He do about Democrats lying about Republicans and Republicans calling Democrats names? What would He do about same-sex bathrooms and gender-identity programs force-fed to toddlers? Knowing His love for all of us and His desire to protect all of us from exposure to sin, there is an answer to that question.

The bigger question is: What will *you* do if that answer is not the one you want it to be?

IDENTITY
POLITICS

A victim really has no identity except that of victim! We are engaged in an inner war with our personal life circumstances and our spiritual condition. That's why, sadly, a victim's identity is always blurry and confused. He struggles to see God's truth about himself.

My inability to see God's truth about me as a young woman led me into all the wrong arms. Inside myself, at war with my own demons of sexual abuse, low self-esteem, pride, anger, and fear, I could never accept that I could *choose* victory. How can you make that choice when nothing about your life says you are a victor? I get it. You can only experience the truth you feel in your emotions and the truth that screams loudest in your diseased mind.

Controlling its citizens is the aim of a politically broken nation. Control is necessary in order to avoid a rebellion against big government and hyper-liberal ideology in the political war zone. In fact, a rebellion in the political war zone is likely to occur when citizens become independent thinkers. To allow citizens to be independent thinkers, forming their own identity, is scary because it could very well mean a shift in the status quo—and *that* means those in power get shifted out of their powerful positions! One thing all leaders need is followers. One thing leaders don't wish to give up is power. And if your eyes are open, you'll see power corrupts in a bipartisan manner.

Sadly, if you look around our nation and many others, it is clear that politicians and parties prefer for all of us to live with distorted emotional truths because this keeps our identity confused. They want us to view life through the lenses of anger, blame, hatred, and division. Discovering *identity* is dangerous to the status quo because it is about discovering yourself and your ability to choose victory. You are not under any political system's control when you know your identity. Circumstances cannot control you. People cannot control you. Identity is power in the hands of the one discovers it. This is why Christianity is under attack like never before. Discovering and walking in our identity is the very essence of the Bible; it is your instruction manual for identity. It's who you are. It's the Creator's explanation of *you* to you. Whether you believe it or not, I challenge you to read it. All of it. Then let's discuss your identity and the liberation of your mind to think in a manner extremely different from how you're currently conditioned to think.

When you discover your real identity, it gets harder and harder to shake you from your tree. Your family ridiculing you cannot shake you. Your friends distancing themselves from you cannot shake you. Your fans vilifying you cannot shake you. Your voting ballot may change, and your political views may have to change, but you cannot fight the change that spiritual clarity brings you.

As your life reflects the identity found in fighting for victory in your personal and spiritual war zones, you certainly won't mind being publicly ridiculed. Last I checked, they did the same to Jesus.

But why such attacks on others, like Kanye West, whose identity causes them to stand up for things you don't believe in? *Because they're wrong,* you say? OK, but even if *they* are dead wrong, can *you* be at peace? If not, you're the one with the problem. In fact, I will state that if your identity is so fragile that the journey of another human being through the various war zones they must fight in to choose victory affects you, then you need to shore up your beliefs.

For example, at this stage of my life, my faith is set in stone. I am solid. I am a believer in Jesus Christ as my Lord and Savior, and I live life from a Kingdom mindset. I believe in lifestyle Christianity. I am not threatened or thwarted by my friends or enemies who don't believe or who believe to different degrees. It doesn't concern me or make me angry because others' lifestyles reflect different beliefs and values than mine. Why should it? I know who I am. Your politics only concern me when you tell me I am *wrong* for having thoughtfully arrived at the conclusions underlying my beliefs and political views.

The battle in my own war zones to emerge victoriously, choosing victory over poverty of the mind and hopelessness, has been sufficient for me. To battle for or against others to make choices only they can make is not your task. In choosing victory for your life, you don't get to judge what victory in another person's life looks like. You don't understand his or her personal war zone circumstances or spiritual war zone consequences enough to judge him or her. It is difficult to comprehend the identity struggles and what has caused them in others. But while you shouldn't *judge,* you must try to *understand.*

Sadly, rather than trying to *understand* others, it's easier to sit by doing and saying nothing while safely nestled amongst the status quo. No risk. No need to worry about anybody disliking you or suffering the consequences of speaking up. However, we all know the only thing necessary for evil to triumph is for good men and women to do nothing. That alone makes me assume that in America today, either many good men are doing absolutely nothing or there are no more good men.

To choose to live in the status quo, not thinking or educating yourself on all sides of issues equally, is weak and lazy and rather disgusting to me. It's everything wrong with America today. It's victim thinking and living at the highest. Oddly, many very successful and famous people think and behave like victims, misusing their platforms and speaking from ignorance rather than intellect. They are influential because they look so glamorous and solid on the outside that people listen. This is the problem with a nation that judges from the appearance of things like money, clothing, and fame rather than from the wisdom of God.

The one-sided addressing of issues saddens me because we have all been silenced by the politically correct disease that has infected our identity as a country for far too long. It is stifling even our desire to care enough to communicate with each other. Our national identity once was as a people who spoke up for what is right and against what is wrong. We spoke up with respect for our leaders and those in authority. During Vietnam and Watergate, we spoke up.

However, I dare say that identity today has become so strongly tied to the politics of whatever group or social scene you belong to that rarely does anyone emerge a free thinker. Entire groups and political parties have lost their identity and dare not find it again for fear of losing power and position—or invites and dinner reservations.

I live in Hollywood. We have other ways of needling those who have broken free from the thought police to root their identity in different principles and character that may be contrary to the Hollywood community: We just don't hire them.

I love the movie *The Post* starring Meryl Streep and Tom Hanks. It perfectly illustrates a woman who loses her identity and then has to find it again. After losing her husband and becoming the first woman ever to run a national publication, she loses her friends, her social position, and her lifestyle in order to do what she feels is right. She chooses victory over her own need for acceptance.

Again, a lack of personal identity mutates into a lack of identity as a nation. It is made worse by a lack of dialogue about the different identities people choose to embrace and why. For example, I find myself asking a question that has stirred up much tension and debate in the political war zone: Why are blacks expected to vote Democrat?

What happens if you are an African American Christian and you don't embrace some of the Democrats' more liberal, anti-Christian policies? What if you like the idea of America being great? What if you disagree with handing out entitlements to put a band-aid on people's problems, shutting them up temporarily while never really helping them change their lives? What if you are someone who loves our Constitution and believes in small government? What if you believe our country is special and that people should enter it legally and with respect for our laws and citizens?

As a person who lives from a choice to find victory every day in my life, my identity as a woman of God and a woman of color is present in all my decisions. Personally, I cannot choose to align with a political party that chooses a victim's narrative. I do not embrace the wholesale lie that either Democrats or Republicans know what's best for us as people of color. In fact, I believe they know very little of what is best for us and that they don't ultimately care. I, like many people, am usually silent because of the PC disease that forces blacks to accept that Democrats are on our side. Democrats know who we are. The problem is *we* have forgotten who we are. African-American people have an identity crisis, personally and politically, that is heartbreaking. Constantly forcing a victim's narrative on us politically is crippling, degrading, and humiliating.

The PC disease causes many of us not to honor the fact that, as a people, we once prayed our way into freedom time after time. Yet we are now systematically eliminating both prayer and faith. Reverend Martin Luther King was a preacher of the Gospel. Yet, as a nation, we silently accept the rebranding of his identity in small ways, from Reverend King to Doctor King. Don't forget that he was a Doctor of Theology—the study of religion. In short, he was a man of God and a teacher of the Bible. We are always trying to secularize truth because attaching our nation's identity to God is uncomfortable for those who don't believe in the Judeo-Christian values that built this nation.

Marriage among African-Americans and fathers in the home is under attack. Whose fault is that? What is required to choose victory over this tragedy? Our schools are filled with crime. Who should fight back? We have amassed wealth yet sacrificed morals. We have overcome, yet we live below and under. This is the fault of every individual person of color who has chosen to feed on the victim's narrative that attempts to nurture us on a steady diet of entitlements and handouts when we should be fighting for our kids, our marriages, our history, and each other. Hard work and a job well done is not an invitation. It's a command. I believe in a leg up, not a handout. Handouts only disable people.

Democrats do not take care of black people. Republicans do not profess to, but historically and currently, the evidence is shocking that perhaps they do—more than Democrats would want us to think. People should care for each other. Black lives must matter to everyone, but they must first matter to black people. We must be the change we desire to see in our own communities and schools. Yes, it takes time. Many have labored long and hard. But as my dad used to always say, "Baby girl, your road is easier than those who went before you, so complain less and work harder."

We have issues to address as a community of people and a nation of citizens. As my old friend Oscar-winning actor Denzel Washington always says, "Do what you gotta do so you can do what you wanna do."

This is the battle cry for the warrior who chooses victory in the face of everything. Do what you gotta do so you can do what you wanna do. Stop looking to others for political help. "God bless the child that's got her own," my adopted mom Roxie Roker-Kravitz used to say. Getting your own begins with choosing to get up and get away from the victim's narrative that any political leader or party offers you today.

Values like faith, inclusion, and hard work were the values of all those who fought to free not only our physical bodies but our minds from slavery.

Those were my father's values. My dad taught me all about hard work and using your own freedom to think and be whatever you dream—not what a political party dictates. Yet it seems we are not thinking at all in terms of race politics in the political war zone. At what point do we ask ourselves if race is simply how we are controlled? It has worked for decades in countries all around the globe. Keep the racial divide as long as it works to control the voters.

I voted for Barack Obama in his first election, but I laughed out loud when he played the race card in South Africa at a university in 2018. It actually seemed hilarious to me to stir up a race-baiting debate when South Africa has had nothing but black leaders since apartheid ended. How, twenty-five years later, under black rule, can you still blame racism for a country's problems? This is utter insanity and a complete forcing of a victim's narrative to control people. It's tragic to do this to young people rather than helping them understand what *choosing* victory for themselves and their country looks like. Leaders manipulating them into hopelessness and poverty of the mind? It is pure evil.

For lack of vision, people perish. We as grown-ups should be casting a vision of a victorious future for young people, not stapling them to the wounds of the past. One creates victors. The other creates victims. I wonder what race-baiting hatred our former President stirs up in his own home? I would say none. His daughters both attend the most privileged universities in the world, and one has a wealthy white boyfriend. Yet to remain in power, leaders must control the masses, and the best way to do that politically is through race and division.

It's time we take responsibility for ourselves and our actions. It's time we start using our brains to think our way into better education, better housing, and better jobs whether or not we have money, help, or resources. Those are beginning to resemble excuses more than socioeconomic conditions.

It's time we stand up and be the change we want to see in our own communities. I look at ethnic groups that are so good at bonding together and working collectively for change. They live together until they own buildings and work together until they run industries. Yet we as people of color don't.

I don't need the Democrats or the Republicans to tell me how to think or who to vote for. Just as I don't need Black Lives Matter to represent me in knowing that black lives *do* matter. *All* lives matter. But black lives have to start mattering enough to us as black people to stop letting any political party dictate who we are and what we should think, do, be, and accept. If the Democratic Party holds a position of unquestioned power in your life simply because you are African-American, you should sit down and check yourself.

Black America was formed on the backs of enslaved Black America's prayers, hard work, and freedom to dream of a better life. The guide we used to have when we sang spirituals in the cotton fields and imagined freedom in our minds made us figure out things like the Underground Railroad and birthed a nation through men who found a way to get educated, no matter what.

It's never too late to ask the Janet Jackson question of your political party. "What have you done for me lately?" Since when did hope become Republican? We should all want America to be great! And we will all be great when we become unafraid to choose victory and reject the victim's narrative that political parties use to control us.

Our political war zone is bitter because we have become bitter people who have lost their way. If your party lost, get over it with dignity, and support the side that won. It's *our* America. If your side won, don't be prideful—just do a great job. It's *our* America.

Whatever a political party once provided me, I long ago began to refute its value and validity. My voting must now line up with the God-given compass that directs me and the baseline morals that ground me. If you ground your identity in the promises of God over your life, you won't need to ground yourself in your mood swings, your attitude, or your political party for your future. It is He who is faithful. Nobody else.

That's victory you can trust.

MISERY LOVES COMPANY

There is usually strength in numbers. That's what groups are about. Most of the groups that have risen to prominence in the political war zone are about victimhood. Victims gathered together can be strengthening, but without a compass that looks in the direction of *solutions*, victims gathered together are just ... victims gathered together! When the numbers are about pain, weakness, and disappointment, there is less strength than there is anger. Anger repels. Anger projects. Anger is toxic, destructive, and ungodly.

We have seen tons of all of the above. Sadly, this is why many of the groups today like Black Lives Matter, Time's Up, Me Too, etc. will fade away unnoticed if they don't begin to let go of anger through forgiveness and focus on solutions and healing. In the Black Lives Matter movement, one single word would have changed and united the entire country: the word *"also."* Instead, singularly focused pain and anger created a slogan with an automatic divide.

Groups exist mostly for good motives and with good reason. But sometimes they exist simply to get mad or to get even. The tragic reality is that most often, they are built on the fact that misery loves company. Groups provide a sense of identity, albeit a false one, that brings comfort to each member. "Grouping" is ultimately about victimization and control. Why? Because groups work!

Race, sexual identity, gender, and faith are great ways to divide people into control groups. These groups, sharing a common pain—and often anger or blame—are then easily limited and controlled by the victim's mentality that cripples them. Misery not only loves company, it *needs* company.

All the labels for all the groups that divide us equal one thing only: control of the sheep! Victims make easy sheep. Sheep are easily directed into patterns of thinking and living that suit the shepherd in charge. Sheep follow because we are often in pain. When we feel as if we have been victimized, we tend to band together in a need for commonality and comfort. For identity, if you will.

I joined all kinds of groups to find people I could share my common experiences and pain with. Groups for women of color. Groups for victims of sexual abuse. My friends made up various groups. Girlfriend groups. Guy friend groups. We join all kinds of groups, formal and informal, to find common ground. Within them, it is easy to adopt sheep-like characteristics. Someone is usually the leader of the group. In my case, more often than not, I was. In some cases, men naturally took the leadership role if I relinquished it. (My unconfronted brokenness, acquired by the facts that were part of my personal war zone, often made that impossible. That's an interesting phenomenon. The group identity behavior among men and women is a subject for another book.)

Again, I am cautious in using this description, but I have experienced some of these characteristics in my own behavior and that of others through many years. Consider this summary of sheep from the *Merck Veterinary Manual*:

> Sheep are a prey species, and their only defense is to flee. Sheep display an intensely gregarious social instinct that allows them to bond closely to other sheep and preferentially to related flock members. Flock mentality movements protect individuals from predators. Flocks include multiple females, offspring, and one or more males. Ewes tend to stay in their maternal groups for life, whereas rams may form transient, unstable, and easily disbanded bachelor herds. If most rams in a group die because of fights or diseases, those remaining join another group. Under standard grazing situations, sheep graze together in casual affiliations; social hierarchies are not as apparent as they are for cattle. Flock dynamics are apparent in groups of four or more as evidenced by willingness to follow a leader or flee in unison. Separation from the flock can cause stress and panic. Isolation from other sheep can cause severe stress and should be avoided. Mirrors can be used in the absence of other sheep.

It's uncanny, but victims tend to form groups, or be grouped together by leaders, for convenience and control—especially in the political war zone. Groups tend to behave like sheep. Sheep are conditioned to follow and to flee in unison. In fact, they experience "severe stress and panic" when separated from the group.

The fact that mirrors can be used in the absence of other sheep is also interesting. Sheep seem to require the comfort of others who look like them, even if it's just one other sheep. Basically, you can fake for one sheep the comfort of others by allowing them to merely see an image of themselves. This makes me think of the groups I mentioned earlier. The comfort found in knowing someone else was sexually abused or discriminated against based on race is real. Seeing yourself and your condition in another human being can provide great peace.

However, the problem occurs when what it takes to control the sheep or the group is deciphered by people with less-than-savory motives. Once a leader realizes he can manipulate the group and its tendencies, the prospect for selfishness on the leader's part arises. When the leader can provide fake comfort or the pretense of safety in numbers, the sheep are no longer in a safe haven; they are in a dangerous pasture, possibly following the wrong leader.

None of this is to say that sheep are stupid. They aren't. Sheep, in actuality, are likely to be more intelligent than generally regarded. They respond readily to food calls, may solve problems, learn their names, carry packs, and can even be clicker trained.

People who congregate in groups for identity, shared experience, and comfort are usually intelligent people. They realize what they need. They understand a bit about their offense. They have joined the group to seek some sort of retribution or repayment for what has been done to them, even if that retribution and repayment is only for the satisfaction of being able to communicate or be heard.

I am not making the assertion that people are stupid or that victims or groups of victimized classes are stupid. What I am saying is that these groups and classes are in danger because they are easy prey for predators seeking control. They are clear targets for leaders who have selfish agendas, usually power. Because misery loves company, once you follow the group as your norm, you have chosen, knowingly or unknowingly, to behave in a manner that will allow you to be herded along at the whim of the group leader.

So, let me ask you, what if your group leader is evil? What if he or she is steeped in his or her own agenda and not that of the group? What if all you are to your group leader is one of the numbers he needs to advance causes that have little to do with the misery and pain that has grouped you together with a bunch of other sheep?

Do you really know the shepherd who's in control?

The Shepherd in Control

Sheep, as I mentioned earlier, will naturally look to be shepherded. We as citizens naturally look to our leaders to lead. It's not an overstatement to say that in the political war zone, leaders seem more interested in controlling than in leading. Controlling America politically, however, means politically controlling *you* and *me*!

Whether the sheep are ignorant, or, more often than not, simply deceived, it is important to know that choosing victory for your life will often include your need to rebel against bad shepherds and bad group politics.

People stuck in victimized thinking are easily controlled politically—if not by their own impoverished thinking, then by political parties that create a world filled with constant fear, anger, and hopelessness. This accurately describes our current political arena, in my opinion. We are fed a daily narrative of fear, anger, and division. While I believe it started on the Left because of a childish inability to lose with grace and wear your shock with decorum, it is also now part of the rhetoric on the Right.

Fearmongering leaders keep victims huddled together, afraid to move out of the group no matter how wrong its dynamics may be. They foster the belief that protection only exists within the group and that they, as leaders, are the only ones who care. They make themselves saviors, and the sheep follow. Nobody deserves a savior more than the millions of victims of all kinds of atrocities, big and small, around the world. However, I dare say there are not many human beings that rise to the level of good men, much less savior.

Creating an environment of fear for others is the ultimate victimization. What kinds of leaders do this to groups of people in pain? Who would take advantage of the already disadvantaged? Bad leaders. They do it all the time.

Good shepherds lead well because they care about the condition of the group and each individual in it. Bad shepherds lead wrongly because they do not care about the condition of the group. They especially don't care about the individual members of a group because, apart from their membership, each individual is useless. Bad leaders care about their own condition. The group's power lies in being a group, and that group exists to serve the shepherd. Sadly, sheep will follow a leader over a cliff.

So what exactly is leadership? It's influence! Anytime you are in a position to influence thinking, behavior, or the development of people to accomplish a goal, you are in a leadership role. The question then becomes: how will you lead? And what is your motivation to lead?

My biggest heartbreaks have come at the hands of bad leaders. Leaders who didn't know how to lead and, worse, lacked the correct motivations for it. They were self-serving, not God-serving or people-serving. They used their influence to fulfill personal ambitions. In fact, in bad shepherds, you will notice a fair amount of ego (which typically stands for Edging God Out). These bad leaders have chosen pride and seek to please men so that they will speak well of them and esteem them higher than they are.

Good leaders seek to develop and maintain respect and trust. They know that respect from others comes through honesty, integrity, truthfulness, and wise counsel, to name a few. They know that love and respect are not automatic—they are earned.

Good leaders value their good name because they know trust is developed over time but can be quickly lost and is difficult to restore.

Good leaders know that the greatest Shepherd is Jesus. Leading like Jesus is their goal. The two key elements to leading like Jesus are forgiveness and grace. *Forgiveness* asks us how we respond to the mistakes of others. *Grace* is not being harsh but compassionate when we do respond. These two elements must be grounded in an overall desire to first and foremost seek to enhance the well-being of others.

In the political war zone, choosing victory makes it critical to ask yourself if the leaders you follow are servant leaders or self-serving leaders. Are *you* a servant leader or a self-serving leader? What's the difference? *Self-serving leaders* consider their own interests first, above all others. *Servant leaders* consider others first, before their own interests. Jesus came to *serve*, not to be *served*.

Our Jesus Problem

Our biggest problem in the political war zone isn't a Democrat problem or a Republican problem. We have a Jesus problem. We have a morality and values problem, and few leaders desire to confront their own underlying spiritual malaise, much less that of the nation. But we must. Your choice for victory in all of your war zones will positively impact the spiritual illness of our nation. That is the only way it becomes a thing of the past. How?

This occurs when both leaders and sheep remember whom they serve: Jesus. When we choose Jesus and His example of leadership as part of our victory choice, we will in effect choose to serve each other. Service is part of your identity when you choose Christ. In our political war zone, our victory as a nation is better served through leaders who embrace faith with love. We need to hold our shepherds accountable by not blindly following them. Victors are not thought victims. They live according to the Word of God, not human opinion, traditions, or ideologies. Those who move from victim to victor have an established set of principles they live and die by, thereby assuring their success. The fact that we are not instilling this in younger generations will come to haunt us very quickly.

The fruit of great servant leadership is achieved when a leader provides the next generation with the wisdom, knowledge, and spiritual resources to serve their generation. A desire to equip others is always at the core of a good shepherd's heart. I teach my son so he can do for himself. Beware of leaders who want to do for you. They do not have your best interests at heart.

Someone who desires to see the next generation walk in victory will always seek to help them choose victory. They do this by encouraging them to confront their personal and spiritual war zones head on, always thinking and doing for themselves and not looking to others to think and do for them. They will nurture freedom in younger generations to think for themselves and still love them when and if they choose to think differently for a season.

Lastly and most importantly, a good leader will care enough about the long-term condition of the younger generation and the greater political war zone they will fully inhabit one day to seek to make them *uncomfortable*.

While this applies to any age, it is especially relevant to what I see happening in the church regarding an entire generation. I see many leaders putting on a great spiritual show. I see them serving some watered-down, Diet Coke version of a Jesus whose love is easily won and never lost, no matter how you choose to live.

Jesus's love *is* easily won and never lost. Come as you are, and you will find a good and forgiving Father. That is a statement of who *He* is. But it's not a statement of who *you* are. Jesus also says, "If you love Me, you will keep My commands." He tells us we must repent of our sin and then receive salvation and be filled with the

Holy Spirit. The Holy Spirit is the consciousness we need to navigate a sinful world and our sinful selves. He brings us conviction, wisdom, guidance, and joy. The Holy Spirit is an infilling of Jesus's very love for us as His kids. Your love should make you clean yourself up, if you believe yourself to be in fact the temple of God. Your love for Him should make you desire to confront your issues and change. If you are unwilling to seek change and think it's cool to remain as you are, you don't love Him as you may tell others you do. Our love of Jesus on the inside is reflected by outward change. If you prefer to hold onto the sin you know you need to let go of, you are choosing to be a victim, not a child of God.

Many leaders have influence over hundreds of thousands of young people yet don't seek to challenge them with truths that may make them squirm in their chairs. They are men and women who desire their own objectives over the much-needed transformation of the flock they claim to shepherd.

I saw a good shepherd in action recently. I attended a church in Minnesota where the pastor spoke for forty-five minutes on celibacy. Not that this was odd. What was odd was that he was addressing a large group of single members in their early twenties. This was in a well-to-do mega-church. I would have honestly not been surprised to hear a very unchallenging message, if only to get the bills paid. Yet the pastor was risking his own security to preach the truth to young people who probably wanted to hear anything but a repentance-and-celibacy message. The world around them victimizes them daily with compromise on this issue, and they often choose much less than victory according to Jesus in this war zone. Yet here was a man who seemed more like a good father, who *cared* that his kids make it through life truly happy and safe. He wasn't interested in whether they got mad at him or chose not to speak to him for a week. He was interested in leading well, so his choice for true victory was evident: the victory found in the Word of God.

Losing America

We cannot be a nation of overcomers and overachievers until we get over it! Whatever *it* may be! Whatever you're mad at. Whatever you're angry about. Whatever happened to you. Whoever treated you badly. Whoever offended you. Get. Over. It. The dream that is America is lost in the refusal to choose victory and the choice to hold onto *offense*. Whatever your thing is, when you cannot put it down, everybody eventually pays—yourself included.

While we may have problems in America, it is better than the problems in most other places on earth. The refusal or inability of millions of Americans to let go of the problems and challenges that have progressed from limiting them physically to limiting them mentally has made us angry at America and ungrateful she is ours. How have we become a country that hates what God has given us? We are a great land, a mighty nation. America is a place I prefer to come home to over any other place on earth. This is a place that others around the world are dying to get to.

So why do we take her for granted now and act as if her past and current imperfections are in some way a reason to destroy her? Is it because, as the current liberal political narrative reads, "America disappointed us when she elected President Trump"? Is it because the far left is so mad they want you and me to hate America along with them for disappointing us? No matter what has happened in your life, only someone living far below the victory threshold would choose to destroy their own backyard. As my sister always says, don't be so mad you harm *yourself*!

Since when is being a patriot a sin? Since America has failed to provide solutions for people's problems!

Why does it feel as if we are losing America? Because Americans refuse to own their part in not seeking solutions to their own problems inwardly before looking outwardly at their country to fix them. Americans are asking what the country can do for them, not what they can do for the country.

Since America is run by Americans, the ultimate answer lies with "we the people." We the people and our unwillingness to deal with ourselves. We the people and our choices for compromise. We the people and our compromised leaders. We the people and our compromised morals. We the people and our poor choices. We the people who accept everything, to our own detriment. We the people who have become so open-minded our brains are spilling all over the ground. We are, in fact, hemorrhaging victims the way we are hemorrhaging brains.

When you're so angry that you take someone or something for granted, it's not long before you realize you've let that person or thing slip away. The fact that America hasn't provided solutions that bring peace, solved the myriad problems we have internally, ended racism, stopped sexual abuse, and nurtured women's rights enough to please all women is quite simply not America's fault. It's *yours* and *mine. We are America!*

The solutions we need are right in front of us: in the mirror. The solutions begin with each and every one of us choosing victory in our individual war zones, which will collectively bring us victory in our political war zone.

You begin by choosing to fight the hopeless narrative created by personal circumstances, many not your fault. Yes, those personal circumstances have caused you brokenness and fear and anger and defeat. But you must confront forgiveness for everything and everyone that has done you wrong. Let go of the sin that has you tangled up, reacting to pain, living far below what you were created for. Your choice right now to fight for your own victory and let go of feeling as if someone, somebody, the entire nation owes you victory is the only way you will have the *more* you want out of life.

America will never offer you solutions because America is made up of Americans. Americans are merely people. People are unable, incapable, and often unwilling to offer you the solutions you need. Only *you* can offer yourself solutions. The *choice,* whether you like it or not, is yours. But, it is not a *choice* you have to make alone. Jesus is always waiting to help.

THE CHURCH AND OTHER MYSTERIES

As a believer, I ask myself, *Where should the Church be in all this?* The Church has a significant role it can *choose* in changing the PC narrative from simply accepting all victims to raising up nations of victors. The Church should be leading the way in living out God's love. We should be engaged in the messy and inconvenient truths of our nation, just as the slaves kept Jesus at the core of their hope while stuck in the cotton fields of the Deep South. Their songs were the evidence of their hope and the testimony of what a relationship with Jesus will do to elevate the human spirit from victimization to victory.

The Church is best suited to demonstrate that love toward God is not weakness. In a mere hour of unity, the church around the world has the power to make stands that don't include demonstrations of words or violence. I have seen silent prayer change entire communities. In our home alone, we have seen groups of young people unified to pray for each other and watched lives change, limbs heal, and a deaf kid regain his hearing.

Love toward God is anything but weak. It is love that goes only toward self that is the weakest love I have ever seen. In fact, this kind of selfish love is the complete example of victimhood. Some victims are incapable of loving God and others in the way they desire to be loved because they are so steeped in their own need. They go through life like vacuum cleaners, sucking up all they can from the world around them while not really considering the world they are sucking from. It is possible to be a victim and overlook other people as you ask from them, take from them, and never think to inquire how they are. I have lived this one personally.

As parents of a former Kansas Jayhawks basketball player, we found ourselves immersed in a very high-level program, with high-level players, high-level expectations, and even higher-level pressure to perform. We taught a Bible study that had grown in size and reputation throughout the entire state by the time our son graduated. We just wanted to love kids and serve God in our time there. We also wanted our son to play some.

For years, I was surrounded by a variety of people. Some of them became and remain good friends or people I esteem highly, whether I see them or not. Others, often fooled by the size of our home, felt they had less, so they felt we owed them some of the more we had. Feeling bad for anyone in need, we tried to give constantly. In the end, what I learned is that, no matter how much you give when someone has chosen to see themselves as a victim, it is never enough. They will vacuum you dry of your time, your money, your encouragement, your prayers, and your spirit, and never look back at you. There is no way to level the playing field or to apologize enough for your success. There is also no way to give enough, encourage enough, help enough, or fix enough.

We spent many days in conversations with parents who cried because their kids didn't get all the playing time they wanted while ours was benched for an entire game. I gave love and friendship to wives whose husbands instructed them not to be friends with me because I was a "player parent" (whatever that is—something short of a human being, apparently). We spent money, time, and gave God's love in the face of much less than even human kindness at times only to walk away with little, except knowing we had chosen victory for our home in spite of the circumstances that victimized us weekly.

Love is revealed through forgiveness.

This is the love the Church can walk in to change our nation and to heal the political brokenness we see all around us. Nothing short of love revealed through forgiveness will work. As I have tried to illustrate, in dealing with the pain of watching my son become a man in the very competitive and often harmful environment called Division 1 basketball, my love often had to be revealed through forgiveness. Forgiveness of coaches. Forgiveness of parents. Forgiveness of circumstances, decisions, choices, and people.

As believers who make up the body of Christ called the Church around the world, the greatest way we can wage war in the political zone is to reveal our love through forgiveness daily. It is the ultimate victory choice with the greatest results for your life and God's will.

Sadly, human nature is not forgiving. It is human nature to hold wrongs against one another and against God. Mankind loves to blame and curse God for everything under the sun. When the car won't start, when the basketball game is lost, when the house burns down, when the meals are not ready in time, when losing the lottery, when diagnosed with cancer. When there is damage from a volcanic eruption, a tornado, or a tsunami, we all have friends who say, "This is an act of God," "I guess this is God's will," or "Why would a good God allow this bad thing to happen?"

We have all blamed God for the less-than-desirable circumstances we have lived through. It is super easy when you are in ministry to get angry at God for allowing you to go through hurtful things when you are helping others. This is a danger zone for the believer and the church. Let me state it clearly and from experience: Your service to God and your mandate to love others does not mean God owes you anything in return. You may work your buns off helping the poor, listening to their problems, or serving a community while it abuses you, your kid, your views, and your values, but you are not entitled to something special from God for doing what is right. The reward for doing the right thing is that you have done the right thing. As Jesus said, it is more blessed to give than to receive.

If every citizen who makes up the body of believers in the Christian church would simply do the right thing according to what the Word of God says, ours would be a nation of people living from one victor's narrative to the next. Kind of like the Bible says, we go from glory to glory. We would no longer be a nation losing the war for peace, unity, and understanding in its political war zone.

Thought Victims

I do not believe any one man is to blame for the lack of harmony in our nation. It's ignorant to believe that. I don't even believe any one man can agitate me into a place of acting in a manner inconsistent with my beliefs and identity. If I am angry, I will look for any excuse to be angry. If I am filled with hurt, I will look for any reason to express my pain.

Victims constantly blame leaders for their state of mind, their condition of heart, and even their failures. If a president, or any leader or political party, holds that much sway over your emotions, you need to check in with what's really going on inside your mind and heart. There are deeper issues to be confronted and deeper victimizing thoughts at work. To say the least, you have exalted political ideology above God, and the narrative it offers you will never be as powerfully liberating as the one God offers.

Kanye West is famous, in part, for saying outrageous things. The fact that fans who have embraced every outrageous statement he's ever made attack him for supporting President Donald Trump seems completely hypocritical to me. Kanye has said and done several things I didn't agree with in the past. Yet until he began to speak opinions inconsistent with liberal ideology, everything he said and did was embraced.

How is it that nobody thought it was foolishness, even blasphemy, to see an image of Kanye on a cross, making statements comparing himself to Jesus Christ? That ran afoul of what is right for *me*, but so be it. He is free to express himself creatively. But seeing Kanye in a MAGA hat, meeting with President Trump and saying Trump is doing a good job for black people is considered blasphemy? I draw the line. Where exactly on earth have our values and priorities gone? When did the former become OK and the latter not OK? Why is a young black man in America being demonized for daring to express an independent thought? Like his opinions or not, I love that he is independent enough to express them. Sadly, many people do not. He has found his victory in Jesus, and the way he is now expressing his thoughts about his faith is refreshing.

Too many people in our nation are what I call *thought victims*—those who think they are living victoriously because the status quo affirms their every thought. In fact, they all share the same thoughts. They do not realize that all original thoughts have been removed from their heads. They are lazy, researching only the truth in front of them and the truth they desire to see—which is often the truth that makes them comfortable in the social scene they want to belong to. Since they feel they are the majority, they feel their thoughts are affirmed as the only ones that matter. For thought victims, it is usually their way or the highway. They feel enraged and victimized by anybody who dares to think differently. I am sure this is because, deep down, they know they don't have any facts behind their thoughts, other than those selectively provided by the chorus.

When a nation lacks identity, its citizens are easily controlled by making them *thought victims*. This is political manipulation at its highest. Whatever party you belong to, your choice for victory demands that you remain free to choose and to have your own thoughts.

This is why I registered as an independent. I voted Democrat my whole life, when I voted. My Hollywood community demanded it. I felt comfortable with it because I didn't really question anything. My emotions controlled me and fueled my idea of love, so I voted emotionally and not from a place of God's love or wisdom.

When I began to question the world around me—whether there was a God and whether I was in fact part of a different plan than the one I had selected for myself—I began to become more conservative. I wound up at odds with my political party on major issues like abortion. How can you read the Bible and not be?

I began to look in the mirror at my rocker, hippie-chick self and see a girl who realized that reason exists only in the mind of God. And in the mind of God, there are things that are, in fact, wrong. My faith forced me to recognize my own thoughts over the ones supplied by the social group I had lived in my whole life. I knew God loved us all—straight, gay, those who've had abortions and those who haven't. We are all sinners who serve a sinless God. But I also began to think that maybe, just maybe, the instructions in the Bible really are His love letter to us, to be read and taken seriously. God doesn't fall off the throne when we don't follow Him, but we fall into a lesser life than the one He created us for. We essentially *become* victims when we choose our opinions about life over God's. The truth of this nagged at me until I became an independent thinker who moved away from going along with my group to going along with Jesus.

This, of course, has put me in some really uncomfortable situations. I have cried many tears over my own family attacking me over religion and politics. I have brothers whose "tolerance" of my conservatism borders on hatred at times. I have even spent dinners with pastors who have shown me nothing but disdain because they dislike my political views. It is shocking to me, and I often ask, "Where is the love?" But it seems the thought-victim manipulation reaches into every sphere of society, including the church. Why? Because people's pain and brokenness, carried from their personal and spiritual war zones, deeply affect how they process life in the political war zone. Thereby, we have become a nation divided—lacking love, understanding, humility, and wisdom.

There is no ability to respect and admire someone who thinks differently than you do when your core is so broken that anybody with a different viewpoint frightens you. I find it insanely hypocritical that I am not at all afraid of someone's views being radically different than mine, but they are angry and threatened by my views showing up in their presence. Incapable of escaping their own inability to cope with "thought" that is different from their own, many people simply choose to behave as victims, choosing hatred as their weapon rather than victory as their bridge.

I think we all have had friends with whom we would never dare share our faith or political opinions. How sad that we have accepted one-sided relationships as the compromise to true dialogue. The enemy of our unity, as a nation, seeks to destroy our ability to communicate in love with one another in the hopes of finding a place of victory from which we all can live. Victims make better spoils for thought manipulation because, as a rule, those who live with a victim's mentality are confused about identity or lack it entirely.

Nobody was more confused about her identity than I was. Yet I knew I had the choice to define myself as a victim or a victor. You do too!

LEGISLATING RIGHTEOUSNESS

Since much of my answer to how you choose victory and move from victim to victor is rooted in choosing Jesus, I would ask whether or not we can, or should, really legislate righteousness. How do any of us teach people what righteousness is when most of us are so sinful?

Can we help heal our broken political soul by forcing a belief system onto others that they may or may not want? Should we even try?

America has scriptural foundations all through it. Visit Washington, DC, and walk around our monuments. Our foundation is influenced by the beliefs of our Founders. I will go so far as to say that we need to fortify those foundations once again. That's why the evangelicals in America like Trump. Simply put, he defends the Church and the rights of Christians to be Christians. We want to be left alone to our faith, the way every other faith comes here and demands to be left to theirs. Yet as testimony to our brains falling out of our heads, we do it for them but not for ourselves. Why?

I believe the answer is simple. The truth of God and righteousness is terrifying to those who don't believe and to those whose belief has grown cold. Truth is a mirror that when reflected back at us provides knowledge of what's really there. That mirror can only reflect truth. Whether you like what you see or not is irrelevant. You will choose to be offended, and immediately run and hide, or seek to smash the glass and destroy the mirror. Or you will love what you see and appreciate that the mirror is showing you where you need to improve. Truth offends, affirms, encourages, shames, or scares. It does many things to many people. But the one thing it cannot do is lie. It cannot because it is the Truth. The face you see in the mirror, for better or worse, is you.

But I also say this: None of us, no matter what we believe, can force our beliefs on others. It just won't work. The choice for Jesus and living a life submitted to Him must, by its very definition, be a free one. Otherwise, it isn't love.

So the question then becomes: can we legislate morality and righteousness *without Jesus*? Are biblical morals supposed to influence broader society? How and to what extent? Is our job as Christians to work in society toward this end? If we made more laws to influence people, even non-Christians, toward biblical morality, would our society in fact become more moral?

Legislating righteousness or morality is ineffective because, sadly, legislating moral behavior doesn't actually change people. Only Jesus does. In fact, since He alone is our righteousness, any attempt at legislating righteousness or morality only makes people look like they are changed when in fact they aren't. Because it's not real change.

As Christians, we have to ask what we are really after. Do we want people to *look like* they are changed by Jesus, or do we want people to actually *be* changed by Jesus?

Do we want to encourage people, albeit unintentionally, to have a form of godliness but reject, or not understand, the power of Christ that actually transforms their lives?

Faith in Jesus precedes following the commands of Jesus. Following Him, or anybody else, for that matter, doesn't lead to an automatic baptism of faith. On the contrary, forcing someone to follow what they don't understand or accept is quite possibly damaging to them.

Back to my favorite scripture: "Without faith it is impossible to please God because those who come to Him must first believe that He exists and that He rewards those who diligently seek Him." Righteousness and morality is something that Jesus works in our lives from the inside out, not the other way around.

God doesn't look at the outward appearance but at the heart. He does care about the "outward" in that He cares about our actions and the kind of lives we live. But a heart can't become righteous through externally imposed rules and regulations. A heart can only become righteous through the transforming work of Christ in a person's life. A righteous lifestyle will overflow from a heart that is growing in righteousness as a person walks with Jesus. The outward appearance naturally looks different when the heart is first right.

Jesus had a ton of influence. He was and still is the most influential person to ever live. Whether you accept Him as your Lord and Savior or not doesn't negate this fact. But Jesus, unlike other leaders, rejected political influence when He was on this earth. Why? Because that wasn't His chosen method to further His Kingdom in this world. He explicitly said in John 18:36 that

His Kingdom is not an earthly one. When people tried to make Him their king, as seen in John 6:15, He escaped the crowds, leaving them to their notion of what a king should be. He couldn't be bothered.

Instead, Jesus taught us to preach the Gospel to every person, in the power of the Holy Spirit, and teach believers to obey His commands. That's how people *come* to faith in Christ and it's how they *grow* in faith in Christ. This was Jesus's directive. Faith is not found through legislation or through Christian morals influencing politics. Nor is it through Christianity being the dominant culture-shaping voice in society. These are man-made goals. They are worthy goals. But they are not Jesus's goals for calling people into faith.

Not that we should promote lawlessness or allow people to rob, steal, or kill without repercussions. It's pretty clear that there is an inherent moral quality in making some things legal and some things illegal based on their impact on society. Even if all people don't agree on where that moral standard comes from, we get that some laws are moral in nature. But are laws God's primary method of producing morality and change in people? No, they are not.

On the other side, here is the dangerous thing about *not* legislating righteousness and moral behavior. Standards of morality and righteousness in the world can change according to people's subjective judgment absent Jesus. In the 1950s, we began never seeing married couples on TV sleeping in the same bed. Now we see unmarried sex on TV between men and women, women and women, and men and men all the time. Without a heart change as to right and wrong being based on God as the author of right and wrong, there is no reason someone would understand how evil this progression really is. You cannot tell a child not to steal because it's immoral without explaining that the standard of immorality comes from God. If you do, who's to say he is wrong when he determines for himself it is moral and righteous to steal—or even kill, for that matter? Situational ethics always lead to one conclusion: there is no God.

Pornography falls in this gray area of accepted moral behavior. Now that it's legal, people try to legislatively protect those involved in it when it wouldn't even exist if we understood God and His design for sex. I believe pornography should be illegal because there are zero deeper, meaningful, intellectual, or spiritual reasons to allow it. There is more harm done than good in allowing the flesh to be fed on pornography.

Sadly, in a culture whose moral standards have shifted, the laws have shifted as well. There are more porn channel offerings on my TV channel guide than faith or morality or even family channels. It should be criminalized for the damage it does—not just to the participants but to the innocent bystanders.

Legislating moral behavior in this way would minimize damages, for sure. But it wouldn't alleviate the deeper spiritual problem at the root of our condition. If all sex outside of marriage was made illegal, it still wouldn't cure the mind that is so seared by sin it needs to see twisted sexual images repeatedly, nor would it change the heart toward repentance and faith in Jesus. Keep in mind, many forms of sex outside marriage already are illegal—and still, the United States leads the world in sex trafficking, according to a State Department report released last summer. Though it might curtail easy access, outlawing pornography wouldn't automatically make a man sexually pure and morally righteous because he couldn't legally watch sin. Only loving your Savior will do that.

Jesus does have a Kingdom, but it is not furthered through earthly political systems. His Kingdom is formed in the hearts of people as they believe in His Gospel, repent of their sins, and turn to Him with their lives. When Jesus returns, He will establish a physical kingdom that is filled with God's righteousness on this earth (2 Peter 10:13).

For now, however, we as Christians need to be less concerned with whether our faith has the most influence on legislation and more concerned with whether our faith is influencing nonbelievers to fall in love with Jesus because we live our faith sincerely. Your walk is so much greater than your talk. We are called to be a light shining in the darkness. The best witness of a powerful God is your powerfully changed life seen by all those you come in contact with. Only then will you truly be a partner with Jesus to tell people about Him and see them brought into His family.

Your change matters. Your submission to Him matters. *He can't save you if He can't command you.* When you look appealing and whatever you're doing is attractive to others, they want it. Victory worn in this way is a reflection of the victorious choices on the inside. It's not legislated. It's real. In a world searching for authenticity, your real power is in the victory in your real life. That victory is Jesus.

Jesus's intention is not that people be pressured to follow His commands regardless of whether they have surrendered their lives to Him or not. His commands are not meant to be followed apart from personal faith and relationship with Him. When you separate morality from the Author of it, you end up where we are today. We live in a society where morality is relative and righteousness is thought to be achieved in actions, works, and various forms of charity. But righteousness is not about your works, your efforts, or your charity.

When our God-given assignment as Christians is to be messengers of reconciliation with God but our methods are pushing people away from Him, there is a big problem.

I love Charles Finney. His writings are so in-your-face and honest about our lack of *real* love for our fellow man. Legislating morality partly stems from this. Because we want someone else to do our job, it helps us feel more comfortable that we are not seeing people come to Christ.

Worse still is that to legislate righteousness is to make Jesus's free gift of dying on the cross a joke. *He* is our righteousness. Apart from Him, we are not righteous, nor can we be. The Bible deals with that bit of prideful thinking by explaining that our righteousness is like filthy rags! All have sinned and fallen short of the glory of God, so get over yourself.

We are in the world but not to be like it, according to Scripture. We cannot live completely separated from people who don't share our beliefs. Nowhere in the Bible are we told to live in a bubble. But how do we navigate an entire political war zone with such fundamental differences? In short, by respecting and loving others, by turning the other cheek occasionally, by exercising Godly wisdom, and by understanding God's position on all this.

Our Constitution gives all citizens the rights of free speech, freedom of the press, freedom to practice our respective faiths, or freedom not to practice any faith at all. These rights don't only apply to Christians. Sadly, by the way some Christians react to people doing and saying things that are different than our beliefs, we appear to be hateful and non-inclusive. This has to stop. Whatever ground Christianity has lost in our political war zone has to be retaken with wisdom, love, and Jesus.

God doesn't agree with sin or rebellion against Him at all. There are eternal consequences for sin against God. The door is open to every person to come as they are, sin and all. Every person, however, has to respond to His call by their own *choice*. Again, we can choose victory, but following Him is another choice.

Jesus interacted with people who didn't yet believe in Him or follow His commands. So we as Christians should interact with people who don't share our beliefs or practice our faith—not just to convert them. I have many relationships in which I have planted seeds and sown Christlike love for many years simply because it's who I am and it's the right thing to do. Jesus preached the Gospel to people who didn't know Him. He called them to leave their sin and follow Him, but He also shared meals and conversation with them along the way.

If you remember well, the Pharisees, who were the religious leaders of the day, didn't like this at all. They questioned the disciples about why Jesus ate with "such scum." Jesus came to the defense of the "sinners" and rebuked the ones who thought their religion gave them the right to look down on "outsiders."

I love this because it shows how you can get so caught up with religion for religion's sake that you completely miss the heart of Jesus and the purpose of what He wants to do in the lives of people.

He expects us to bring His healing into this world so He can restore people's broken relationships with Him. We can't do that if we're busy hiding from them or trying to sanitize everyone who is different from us solely for our own comfort. When we do that, we're no better than those Pharisees.

We are Christ's representatives in this world. We are as good as it gets, and that's not so good on many days. But we can't afford to make the mistake the Pharisees made. He loves everyone, even while they are still in rebellion against Him. That's Bible. He is working to reconcile people to Himself, not condemn them and push them away. That's Bible too, folks. It's also victory. Choosing victory negates the need to legislate righteousness and moral behavior when choosing Jesus is the ultimate victory choice.

Everything about the way we treat people who don't share our Christian faith should communicate His end game, not ours. Everything about the way we interact with people should communicate Jesus's heart to love and reconcile people to Himself. That includes lovingly and graciously speaking the truth of His message *and* having meaningful relationships with people as we do it.

Jesus established a much better way of legislating righteousness and moral behavior. He died for our sin so we could be righteous before God. And the good news of Jesus is still the power of God for victory and salvation for anybody who chooses to believe.

I Forgive You Collectively

There will always be much I can say about forgiveness in any war zone where you are fighting. Forgiveness is the greatest key you hold to unchaining yourself from the weight of sin and releasing yourself into victory.

"Father, forgive them, for they know not what they do," Jesus said. He was speaking about the soldiers at the cross just as much as He was speaking about the nation. People don't fully comprehend the depths of their actions. If they did, they wouldn't choose to remain stuck in victimization. In closing out our look at various elements we face and how to overcome them in our political war zone, I hope a vision of a better America can be seen. We are a great nation because we are composed of people who have it within them to be great.

John Adams said, "Our Constitution was made only for a moral and religious people. It is wholly inadequate to the government of any other."

So do we change our Constitution, or do we change as people?

I submit that we change as people. But that happens only through embracing the wisdom in which I present forgiveness to you. It begins in a choice for morality—not separate from God but authored by God. We cannot legislate righteousness. We cannot legislate morality. But we can forgive those who have sinned against us and choose to move forward in forgiveness—a quality most like Jesus. There is great victory in our shared political war zone for you, for me, and for us all through forgiveness. A broken nation looks like one that has divided into groups, calls each other names, spreads lies in the media, and spews hatred for people. A great nation looks like one that has forgiven the sins of its past to embrace the glory of its future.

I choose victory for America. I believe that when America chooses forgiveness for its past, it will find victory for its future. This collective choice must be made by you and me!

PART IV:

The Victory Zone

PERSONAL RESPONSIBILITY

So you have arrived in the victory zone. You have chosen to move from victimization to victory! But how? Are there really people who've done this? Yes! Some of today's greatest success stories have come through pasts riddled with inequality, abuse, and victimization. Some of the victors you see today are yesterday's victims who made the same choices I am asking you to make.

People who've chosen victory are more powerful than those who haven't. A victor encourages victory everywhere he or she goes and with everyone he or she comes in contact with.

Remember Lori, the little girl whose father was addicted to porn? Before understanding that victory was a choice that was hers to make, she was doomed to live out the victim's narrative that played over and over in her mind. The subsequent rapes, the abortions, and the sexual sin that were part of the victim's narrative in her personal and spiritual war zones served to affirm her inability to live a "normal life." Her hopelessness would have been perfectly accepted and understood by any of us. Her victimization left her with worse than even poverty of the mind—it left her with a diseased mind.

But God.

At age twenty-seven, Lori met a man of God who had chosen victory for his life. He understood victory. He walked in victory. He was pure and waiting for sex on his wedding night. He had never seen pornography and certainly never desired it. Because of his example, she chose Jesus. She chose to try it His way and found Him faithful. Lori has now been married for twenty-five years, with two amazing, intelligent daughters, in a godly home, serving Christ as a successful woman of God.

The choice to not live according to the narrative written for her in her personal war zone was hers to make, and she made it. The choice to go to war with her flesh, corrupted not just by the sin of others but eventually by herself, was her battle to fight, and she fought it. She chose forgiveness. She chose victory. She chose Jesus. She calls that the best choice she's ever made.

I often think of young people who become victims of tragic accidents, such as Bethany Hamilton. The film *Soul Surfer* is about Bethany. In it, we meet a teenage girl with a great life. She has awesome parents, great friends, and incredible opportunities in front of her. After a tragic shark attack that took her arm and nearly her life, Bethany was ready to give up on life. She was broken, depressed, and angry. Her whole life plan was altered by circumstances beyond her control. She had a typical victim's backstory.

Yet I wanted to jump for joy when, in the film, you see her in Haiti helping children whose lives were devastated by the hurricane of 2007. She begins to realize how little these children have.

Small children whose parents are now dead, with their homes washed away, begin to paint a clearer picture of her own reality. Bethany begins to realize that she can live her life as a victim or she can find forgiveness for God, gratitude for her blessings, and figure out how to take what she has and turn it into victory. She chooses victory. As a believer, she finds her way to her life's purpose and calling.

Bethany today has inspired millions of young people worldwide who are going through challenging and horrendous situations. She encourages them to choose victory and to never allow a victim's mentality to dominate their lives.

Then there's Denzel Washington, whom I have known for many years. One day, he commented that most of the starring roles he has had were actually written for white actors. He simply chose not to be deterred and made them his own. This impacts me still. If he had waited for roles to be created for him as a black actor, he might never have become Denzel Washington, the movie star we all know and love. If he had gotten stuck in the discrimination and racism that exists in Hollywood and gotten angry or bitter, he likely wouldn't have charmed us all year after year. Nobody is drawn to anger and bitterness. It's some of the spoiled fruit of a victim's mentality. He chose *not* to be a victim.

As people, we are drawn to winners, and usually, winners are problem solvers. We all like problem solvers because we all have problems we need to solve. Denzel solved the problem of not enough roles in Hollywood for black leading male actors for himself. How? By not seeing himself as a black male actor in terms of choosing scripts but by seeing himself as a man capable of playing any role he wanted. We all want to live our lives with a victor's mindset. We want a victor's story. So we are naturally drawn to those who recreate narratives and re-tell their life story in a way that wins.

I carry this lesson from Denzel with me daily. It has inspired me continuously to live from a place of freedom. I share it to remind you that whatever you think you can't do because of the color of your skin, you need to look again. There is likely someone else who has chosen to just do it.

Own Your Stuff

One of the greatest strengths found in those who reach the victory zone lies in taking personal responsibility. Victory is about *you* getting real with *you*! Possibly the most critical part of your victorious choice lies in how well you *own* your own messes and take personal responsibility for your current situation. Even reading this book is about taking inventory of all you can do to change your life. You have a choice, and hopefully, you are making it by simply getting to this point in the book!

Sadly, people who live as victims often destroy things. They destroy their neighborhoods and communities. They destroy themselves. They destroy others. And then they refuse to own their part in the destruction.

I wonder constantly why people destroy the little they have. Yet it happens. Sadly, poverty of the mind causes many people, because they live in poor neighborhoods or modest communities, to accept garbage and graffiti and broken glass lining their streets.

But people who have chosen victory build up their neighborhoods and communities, encourage themselves and others to make a difference, and own their part and what they can do to eliminate destruction!

After my parents' divorce, we lived in a community that has truly changed through the years. When my mom was young, it was predominantly middle class and white. Thirty years later when my mom moved us back there, I was a teenager, and she was a divorced woman with six kids. It was on the edge of a completely different South-Central LA experiencing issues with gang violence and drugs. Today, in the midst of regentrification, it is a mixed-race, middle-class neighborhood with skyrocketing prices.

Through all of this, my mom tells me she never waited for anyone to keep our neighborhood clean or safe. She never sat around wondering why the city didn't do certain things. She never stopped at complaining that more city resources would keep the gangs off our block, keep the walls of local markets graffiti-free or the alleys uncluttered by junk and litter. She took responsibility for her block. She took personal responsibility to *be* the change, and she was never angry about it. She felt it a joy to have a roof over our heads. She was often picking up outside after neighbors, moving their trash cans in and out if they didn't do it themselves. She persistently called the city to be sure the streets were repaired when needed. She brought victory to the lives of every person who lived on our block because she refused to think and live like a victim. She chose victory over believing her environment could be better only if everybody who owed her something came through.

Sometimes a victim's narrative screams so loudly in your head that you decide to block it with drugs and alcohol. Many people are hurting and in despair. I have been there. But it is pointless to destroy your own life.

Particularly when dealing with addiction, I see a tremendous lack of personal responsibility. Not everyone can get help. But many people can. It's true that life isn't fair. People often don't really care. But somebody does, and will. When you dig into a place of victory, you persist until you find that someone who will. God never leaves anyone stranded and unable to get help. No matter how much evil is on the earth, there will never be a complete absence of loving and caring people who will help if you just persist in your quest to find them. He is faithful. A victor takes personal responsibility for needing to *choose to keep choosing* victory until he or she finds it.

Victors assume responsibility for their own happiness. They take personal responsibility to fight for their own freedom. They are persistent. They know they need to participate in their own rescuing. They know that, when they are at the end of themselves, they need God to take over. And they let Him.

Break Bad Habits

We all develop habits, good and bad. Habits are the foundation of our everyday lives. We build our daily practices, and eventually, our habits and routines shape us. Victory is found in your habits.

We either build good habits that support us as we move toward our goals or bad ones that undermine our ability to choose victory. You will find it really difficult to overcome your personal war zone, live above your spiritual war zone, and achieve your dreams if you are living with a slew of bad habits. In the victory zone, you need to know if any of these destructive habits are holding you back from your ultimate success and your final victory.

Here are some good habits I've developed along my journey.

Don't Seek Approval
You will never choose victory while seeking approval and permission to choose it. Stop focusing on what others think or say. Listen to your choice and to God, who affirms your choice for victory in countless ways. Your attempts to gain approval from others will only hold you back. There are times when it's good to get others' opinions, but you don't need constant accolades from everyone around you. Know who you are. You don't need approval or permission from any group you may belong to. Seek only guidance and approval from Him and the standards He approves us by.

Set Goals
Defining your goals is the first step toward making them happen; it creates a roadmap that will guide you. Without a plan to pull you

into the future, you can easily drift off course without even knowing it. Victims rarely plan, because they are rarely told they have a future to plan for. If that is you, I want you to snap out of it. You have a future. No matter what your personal war zone looks like and no matter how much sin has entangled your life, He knows the plans He has for you, and they are good (Jeremiah 29:11)!

Stop Doubting

Self-doubt is a dream killer. Negative thinking and a fear of rejection will only fuel feelings of uncertainty and indecision. If you constantly doubt yourself and question whether your goals are attainable, your pessimistic feelings will become self-fulfilling prophecies. Don't let yourself get stuck in a negative thought loop. That is only choosing to sabotage your own dreams and future. You cannot choose victory if you are holding yourself back with self-doubt. Encourage yourself with what God says about you. He says incredible things about your beauty, your worth, your intelligence, and your ability to succeed. Don't doubt yourself because you don't ever need to doubt God at work in you, for you, and through you.

Procrastination Is a No-No

Procrastination is the quicksand of accomplishment. Victims allow themselves to get easily distracted and suckered into inaction and complacency. Failure to keep moving forward in victory will lead to stagnation while inaction will lead to a very active victim's mentality. At some point, victors stop planning and start doing.

Never Feed Distraction

Let's face it, there's never a lack of things to distract you; hello, social media! But when your attention is pulled in a million directions, it's hard to focus your thoughts. If you are living a distracted life, your goals are being sidelined. Stop feeding your distractions. Distraction stifles your achievements. Take a deep breath. Slow down and calm your mind. Doing this at random moments throughout your day will help increase your ability to continually choose victory over the distractions around you and inside you.

Don't Put Anybody Down *(Including Yourself)*
Victors never put others down. They don't belittle the achievements or beliefs of others. By the same standard, they don't do the same to themselves. In your victory zone, speak victory over yourself and your life daily. Telling yourself "You're stupid" or "You can't do anything right" inflicts wounds that will hold you hostage to victimized thinking. Know when things go wrong, but focus on what went right and what you're proud of. Find the good in those around you. Look for ways to bring yourself and everyone else into the victory zone. How? Use words of encouragement and edification, not words that tear down.

Get Out of Your Comfort Zone
Choosing victory involves taking risks! Stepping outside your comfort zone means taking a leap of faith and inviting the possibility of more failure to your life, which you may already perceive to be failure-filled. But you will never know what victory is unless you try, try, try. The things that have victimized you don't define you: they actually make you capable of much. Many business leaders took radical leaps out of their personal war zones to choose victory: Bill Gates, Richard Branson, Larry Ellison, and Warren Buffet. All of them failed at one point, but none would have been successful if they hadn't pushed themselves to continually choose victory. Remember, with great risk comes the possibility of great reward. You'll never truly move from victim to victor until you try!

Nobody Is Perfect
People who live from a victim's mindset believe they need to be perfect to be included. Nothing could be further from the truth.

Nobody is perfect. Constantly striving for perfection only guarantees that you will constantly feel imperfect. Just as there are areas of your life where choosing victory will be easier, there are area in which you will struggle. You will falter at times and fly at times. Accept that you will make mistakes as you emerge from the victim's mindset that may plague you. Mistakes don't mean you are doomed to live as a victim. Choose to allow your mistakes to strengthen your resolve to change the victim's narrative of your life.

The Time Is Now

There will never be a right time. Victors know the right time is always *now*. Your daily fight in your personal war zone and the sin in your spiritual war zone requires you to not wait but to act decisively and immediately. It is never too late to choose victory. If you never start, you will never succeed.

No Budget, No Matter

The beautiful thing about having been a victim of poverty and many other circumstances is that we all have one thing in common. Most of us never have the money to change everything we wish to change financially in our life. This is why the choice for victory must begin internally. You don't need a budget to make a choice. But you need the choice if you ever want to have a budget. Choosing victory affects your finances, but your finances don't affect your ability to choose victory. One is the cart. The other is the horse. Additionally, victors create good money habits. When you choose victory, you know that money will never define you, just as poverty or abuse or addiction doesn't. Victors treat money wisely and trust God above even their money.

Be Persistent

Persistence is the engine that will get you to the finish line. The ability to stick with your life as a project, working tirelessly to see your battles through, will be your secret weapon to achieve success. Victors are persistent, relentless fighters who never accept defeat. When you have started life knocked down and you have truly chosen to get up, you will never be able to stay down long. In your victory zone, be persistent.

Educate Yourself

Only you can choose how much you know. In spite of your lack of formal education, exposure, or travel, there is a measure in which you can choose to educate yourself. Today, you can get online in a library and teach yourself to read. You can learn about history and architecture and even how to speak another language. If you have never seen the Eiffel Tower, you can experience it online. Don't sit and blame the world for your lack of a good education. Frederick Douglass had it worse than you. He didn't even have the internet! All successful people read voraciously. Reading is the basic way we educate ourselves and gain knowledge. Victors should always be seeking deeper insights. Knowledge empowers your victory choice and will cause you to dream bigger than you would have allowed yourself to imagine as a victim.

Ask Questions

Never think you know it all. The greatest quality of a victorious person is curiosity. I have always been one to ask a million questions. Just as important as asking questions is listening to the answers. Ask questions, but listen intently, deeply, and thoughtfully. Ask to learn!

Own and Apologize for Your Mistakes

Always admit when you are wrong and apologize immediately. Taking responsibility for a mistake will go a long way toward earning people's respect. Victors have confidence in themselves and their choice for victory. Saying "I am sorry" and moving forward establishes your power to eliminate victimized thinking from your life at a rapid pace.

Do Not Be Consumed by Failure
If you are consumed by fear of failing yet again, you likely will. Do not let failing weigh you down. Victors have to continue to take risks, whether it works out or not. You aren't alone. No one succeeds without sometimes failing. Most every victory will reveal a failure along the way.

Live Unentitled
In the victory zone, you have to break any remaining entitlements from your way of thinking. Victims always feel entitled. Victors know that *nobody owes you anything*, not even those who have harmed them. Victors don't expect others to solve their problems or ease their pains; they take personal responsibility for their own well-being. Understanding that nobody owes you anything and that you're entitled to nothing is critical to choosing and living your daily victory. In the victory zone, you live unentitled.

It's Not about You
Understanding that *it's not about you* helps to clear up the world of entitlement you can so easily live in. Today's young people live in a see-and-be-seen society. Of utmost importance is being noticed, affirmed, liked, and friended on social media by masses of people they don't even know.

The number of celebrity suicides that have touched all of us in the media in recent years is a staggering example of this point. Who was *watching* these people? Did anyone *see* or even notice their pain when, after all, they were visible to millions on TV every day? Learning to take your eyes off of *yourself* and put them on *others* is a powerful motivator that helps crush the selfishness that plagues our nation. Truly seeing and experiencing other people, especially those with less than you think you have, automatically drags you into a place of victory. To truly see others, you must do one thing: *Look.* Then you have to *care.*

THE TROPHIES
OF VICTORS

My whole life I, like most people, have wanted to be a winner. I have worked hard to make something of my life that resembles my childhood hopes and dreams. There are seasons of my life I look back on and find that I am quite proud of my accomplishments. There are seasons where I am not proud at all of my behavior or the way I worked out my inner turmoil. But my choice to live from the narrative that sings victory over my days is one I have determined to make daily.

The rewards of making this choice are many. I know who I am. I know why I am. I am thankful for the life I have lived because in the good and in the bad, I have found my identity, calling, and purpose. My history is now His-story.

Happily, I live according to my own authentic compass. I am confident in who I choose to be—and when I change something about myself, I am confident in that change or course correction. As my girlfriend Nina once said to me, "Cyn, you bloom where you're planted." She was right. All victors do. Victims die wherever you plant them because their diseased minds don't allow them to take root in soil they don't recognize. Life will often re-plant you. Will you see that as a blessing or a curse?

I see many people who live bouncing from day to day, never questioning the deeper meaning for their existence. I've never been that way. Even while bouncing, I was questioning. To know why you are here seems a critical goal, and in choosing victory, you begin to understand why. Your victory choice carries a measure of power people want to experience, and that opens doors. Doors to wealth, opportunity, impact, and greater victory!

Along my journey, I've noticed several characteristics all victors seem to have in common. These are the currency of choosing victory. Doors open wide, and opportunity appears in abundance because victors give off an economic energy. You can literally take it to the bank and spend it. That currency is an energy that flows from being clear about your calling and purpose. This clarity is super-motivating for anyone who experiences it. All of these things, and all of the energy that flows, is rooted in one thing: gratitude.

Gratitude

Gratitude is the foundation of all the rewards of victory. You can't choose victory without gratitude, and you can't be grateful without first choosing victory.

Definition of *gratitude*: the state of being grateful: Thankfulness.

There is a light that shines from the victor's soul. That light is called gratitude. Gratitude is so powerful it changes not only you but everyone around you. What does gratitude look like? Why is it so critical in your choice to move from victim to victor, loser to winner?

I get that many people don't see much in their lives to be grateful for. But things could definitely always be worse. Gratitude is established in the heart of someone who chooses to live and walk in victory because it is necessary to understand that no matter how bad things are, you have so much to be grateful for. It is defined as the "state of being grateful," which implies that gratitude is a state of mind you can choose.

In fact, gratitude is a noun. Like my name or your name, gratitude is rather like a tangible being, not just a descriptive adjective. When you live in a state of mind that has chosen gratitude, your victory zone becomes that much more secure. Just as it's your choice to move from victim to victor, the state of mind that will enable that choice day after day, year after year, is gratitude. Think of her, Gratitude, as a tangible being that literally becomes *you*. *There is Cynthia. She is Gratitude in all she does.*

The health benefits of expressing gratitude are many, and some might surprise you. Scholars, spiritual leaders, and scientists throughout history have deliberated on gratitude, and more recently, scientists have validated its effects on both mental and physical health.

Numerous studies demonstrate how gratitude journaling can increase one's happiness. Practicing gratitude boosts the immune system, reduces stress, lowers depression, increases feelings of energy, determination, optimism, and strength, and even helps you sleep better at night. In fact, few things have been more repeatedly and empirically vetted than the connection between gratitude and overall happiness and wellbeing.

As with fasting, it's impossible to untangle the mental and physical benefits of gratitude from its spiritual effects; what is good for the body and mind is good for the soul—and vice versa. At the

same time, the reasons to intentionally practice the spiritual discipline of gratitude radiate beyond these more corporeal effects
to those that more centrally touch one's inner life, moral character,
and even the larger community.

Just as one chooses to practice a mindset of victory, one
chooses to practice a mindset of gratitude.

Becoming more grateful doesn't mean you deny the reality
of life's difficult edges and gut-wrenching sorrows. Instead, while
gratitude recognizes the darkness in our existence, it also notices
the beauty, the joy, the goodness, and the truth that is typically
overlooked. Because of this, gratitude in fact opens one's eyes
to a *more* expansive view of reality. It is like when I finally admit-
ted to myself that I couldn't see as well as I did in my twenties
and put on a pair of reading glasses for the first time. *"Oh, wow,
here's what I've been missing!"* The world became so much clearer.
Through the lens of gratitude, you come to better recognize the
good, to see the many gifts, benefits, and mercies in your life that
might otherwise remain hidden and ignored. Through this lens,
you find strength, joy, and resolve to choose victory over the
despair written in the easier victim's narrative for your life.

Gratitude, arguably the foundation of good character, is a
"parent" of all the other virtues. It counteracts negative vices
like envy, resentment, and greed. When you are grateful for
what you have, you spend less time comparing yourself to
others and less time making poor, fruitless decisions based on
those comparisons.

Second, recognizing that the good in one's life comes, at least
in part, from outside the self develops a vital sense of humility.
It also develops the motivation to reciprocate these gifts, and
return goodness for goodness by practicing more positive virtues.
Striving to do the right thing out of simple duty is great, but duty
is, at best, a mere back-up motivation to joy and thankfulness.
You can grind out living the virtues, but if it's not authentic,

it will feel unsatisfying to you and dry and embittered to others. Gratitude is a fuel that sparks and animates one's courage, generosity, industry, and honor.

It turns our gaze outward so that we are able to see around the victimization we are tempted to cuddle up to and peer into other people's realities. This helps us have right relationship with others. Rather than living narrowly focused on what we lack, we become aware of what we have and what others do to help us. We recognize the human and divine help that's gotten us to where we are today and the help we continue to rely on to sustain our lives. Gratitude allows us to appreciate and affirm the worth and value of the people, structures, and divinity around us rather than taking them for granted.

Studies show that grateful people experience greater feelings of connection and closeness with others and with God. They are more compassionate, less materialistic, more forgiving, generous, and supportive than the ungrateful. The power of gratitude will sustain you in your victory zone when past demons from your personal war zone haunt you and sin from your spiritual war zone tempts you.

I believe the single greatest reward you gain when you war your way into a mental choice for victory is the virtue of gratitude. Gratitude is the supreme trophy of victors.

Supernatural Opportunities and Physical Open Doors

Choosing victory draws an abundance of victories to you! Opportunities that would otherwise be closed to you in the natural spring open when released in the supernatural. It all occurs when the shift inside you is made. Doors begin to open as a result of your choice. People like to be around people who are humble, grateful, kind, and have overcome something. They see people like this as wise. The supernatural energy you give off in your victory zone encourages others to assist you in what they can see clearly as your *calling*.

Your calling is about your ministry (more on this later).

When you walk into a room angry at the world, feeling as if everyone owes you something, I promise you won't get anything except negative results. Your choice to remain a victim will in effect close doors, even supernatural ones, that God has opened for you.

I believe those who choose victory go from glory to glory. Understand what that means. Even the awful things that have happened to you take you from glory to glory when you realize that if you let God take your mess, He makes a message. Your history is truly His-Story when you allow Him in. When you are able to find God in the mistakes and injustices of your life, both you and others will see His glory magnified. Therefore, whether in the good or fighting the bad, God's glory is at work changing, shaping, and cultivating purpose in you. When you realize this, you understand that no matter what is happening in your life, you are simply going from victory to victory. Why? Because He is faithful. But you must choose!

The Economics of Victory

On every level—socially, morally, and politically—it is economically advantageous to choose victory over personal blame, societal blame, and spiritual blame.

Victims seek to drain systems and feel entitled to resources. Yes, that sounds harsh, but this statement is not meant for those with true disabilities and handicaps. People who truly need help do need help. Instead, this statement applies to the millions of able-bodied Americans who hide behind victim groups and wallow in self-pity feeling that God, or somebody, *owes* them a better life than the one they have. This diseased way of thinking causes people to grab at everyone and everything around them as a potential life preserver. They look out at *others*, not up at *God*.

When you are looking for what you can get economically because you feel owed something, our society is put in the position of creating programs and entitlements that only serve to disable the disabled even more. In this scenario, the more that is given to people, the more likely they are to be controlled by the giver. A society that seeks to control people isn't loving or concerned with true prosperity for all. It's one concerned with power and control, which is economically only advantageous to a few.

In the victory zone, you have broken free from control and from feeling entitled. You have likely taken personal responsibility for your economic growth—creating businesses or services that you can offer, trade, or barter for your livelihood. This is good for the individual, and it is good for the nation's economy.

The economic advantages of a nation filled with people who have fought successfully to break the victim's narrative their life circumstances tried to write are tremendous. People in the victory zone are a positive flow into the world around them rather than a negative drain. These people continually seek to grow, not tear down. They look to contribute from their treasure chest of experiences rather than take from others.

The economics of choosing victory are really simple. A *victor* enters a room with a victorious mindset, and we are all drawn to that person's choice. We want to help and participate. A *victim* enters the room, often with legitimate need, and while you may help from pity or a sense of duty, you really don't want to enmesh too much. Over time, the need can simply be too much for most people. I understand this because I have entered many rooms in my life with both of these realities at play. Trust me when I tell you that your bottomless pit of need, despair, and victimization repels people even as they give to you. You don't want this victim's narrative to control your life another day. You were made equal to those around you. You have much to give and contribute—and if you've overcome much, you have even more. Your choice is hugely mental, as are the results you'll experience with others.

The economics of choosing victory as the narrative for your life impact you and everyone around you. *Your* victory zone means *you* have *chosen* to win *your* war. Your choice is a beacon for all who desire to make the choice for themselves and reap the currency they so want for their lives. Everybody profits from a person who has moved from victim, with its negative balance sheet, to victor, with its positive deposits into society.

Your Calling and Purpose

The final trophy I have noticed in the victory zone is clarity about calling and purpose! They are different things but both necessary. When the Apostle Paul started out, he was just an evangelist. He would preach in the synagogue to Jews. He wasn't an apostle. He wasn't a teacher. And he wasn't talking to Gentiles. Yet before it was all over, he called himself all those things. He had other gifts as well, but he knew those other gifts were simply to assist him in his *calling*. His calling was perfected over the years as he grew in Christ.

It's the same for you and me. There is something you know God has imprinted you to do, and eventually, you realize that if you choose victory, you will discover the uniqueness of your identity and the path you alone can walk with Him. If you succumb to poverty of the mind, you will never receive the reward of living out your calling.

Your purpose, as stated before, is simply to love and worship your Creator. That in and of itself is the essence of victory! It is impossible for someone with a victim's mentality to really worship and love God because they live like an orphan with little ability to receive the love of a Father. They do not worship because they don't see anything to be grateful for. Victims don't fully reach their purpose: achieving the elevated mentality of what it means to be a Son or a Daughter of the King.

I receive constant questions from others about how I got to my victory zone. They want to understand how I overcame injustices in my life that would cripple most people.

I have very little problem sharing the things in my life that victimized me because I have chosen to see their value in my calling. I gained strength from surviving sexual abuse so I can now strengthen others. I gained wisdom in God's Word every time I fell down so I am able to help others find His Word and get back up. I worked for years on TV hosting talk shows. Now I use my skill set for communicating information that matters more than make-up tips or fashion labels. Look at your life. You have experiences that others can learn from. Shift the focus off yourself and onto why your life matters to all of us, and you will find your calling!

I see my various experiences, good and bad, as tools in my belt that I can use to lead others into their own victory choice. I shook off their ability to define me, replacing it with my choice to be labeled a victor. I support and understand victim groups and classifications, as long as their goal is to eliminate the word "victim" and replace it with the word "victor."

Choosing victory in this case becomes the cornerstone of calling and purpose. In a support group that is focused on victory, rather than lingering in pain, anger, and blame, you can ask an important question:

What can I do with a life that was attacked, broken, or riddled with undeserved tragedies?

The answer to this question takes on many incredible shapes and forms, dictating tremendous levels of victory to every individual. You can embrace your greatest calling based on the skill set these circumstances have given you rather than great limitation based on their residue.

Think about Paul. When he understood that his whole life was meant to share the Gospel, he was able to do it under any circumstances. He understood his *why*!

What is your *why*? In a world searching to define you by *what* you do, finding out *why* you do it is infinitely more powerful. People will not die for their what. But they will surely die for their *why*! Your *why* is about your purpose. Your *why* can positively impact the whole world. It changes your life, your environment, your community, and your nation for the better.

The most satisfying trophy you receive when you choose to live from a victorious mental state is the *why* behind what God will show you that you alone are equipped to do because of what you've lived through and experienced! The challenges, the pain, the things you've overcome become the fuel for your *why*—and like me, you will come to a place where you wouldn't trade much of your past for the power of your present because of it.

You were created with a unique and victorious offering inside you: an offering that is a gift to the world around you. Everything you have experienced, good or bad, is a weapon in your hand for good—if you choose.

Being able to shift your focus from yourself to all others frees your mind to see the myriad possibilities for your unique, albeit difficult, experience to touch many lives. The mind that lives in victory begins to soar with the eagles, seeing a world from thirty thousand feet, filled with many avenues and flight paths!

Understanding your calling and purpose is undeniably one of the incredible gifts in your victory zone. In my life, choosing victory has unlocked doors and created opportunities that you would have never imagined had you looked at some of the tragic moments, life twists, and burdens I have endured. As the Bible says, count it all joy. What I went through and what you currently may be going through isn't necessarily joyful. I wasn't celebrating while being sexually abused or raped. Cancer wasn't fun or fair. Financial struggles and a season as a single mom on welfare didn't *feel* good. The residue from many of the obstacles that life has thrown me has been hard and painful.

Taking personal responsibility to find the gratitude in my life, no matter what, and accepting that victory is mine to choose and no one else's to give has been the hardest part of my journey. In facing the difficulty in life, you must face the difficulty in each of the awful things that others have done to you, each of the failures and mistakes you have made, and each of the vices and sins you have fallen into. Then you are required to go to war. Yet that war—mentally, emotionally, and sometimes physically—opens many supernatural doors and creates a multitude of opportunities.

Stop living out the narrative that says, "I can't," "I will never …" "There is no hope," or "That never happens for people like me." Stop. Right. Now.

Put on a new narrative. This one says, "I am able. There is nobody else like me. I can do all things through Christ who strengthens me. I am an overcomer. I don't need anything but my faith to push me forward. My God is awesome, and I am His." Repeat it daily.

EVERYBODY LOVES A WINNER

The victory zone is your personal place of celebration and who doesn't love a party?

If you look at it honestly, it's easy to say that everybody, quite simply, loves a winner.

The freedom of choosing victory literally shows all over you. It affects the way you walk, talk, and move. Everybody wants to hang around someone who radiates positivity.

A runner who has run well makes us cheer, especially as they run their victory lap. We give them awards. We give them contracts and deals. We applaud them. We want to be near them. We simply love to be in the presence of winners. It doesn't matter that the race may have been grueling. It doesn't matter what obstacles or hurdles they jumped over along the way. All that matters is the joy we all experience when the object of our attention has won. It's why we collectively love sports. We all love champions.

In the same way, for you who have run the race, it becomes easier to count it all as joy once you've achieved the rewards of your victory choice. You don't consider what you have been through to be greater than where you are because victory is all you now experience. The weight of whatever circumstances you have been forced to carry is no longer a load but the tools that strengthened you to go the extra mile.

"I have fought the good fight, I have finished the race, I have kept the faith" (2 Timothy 4:7 NIV).

I don't suppose there is any sentiment that best expresses what I desire my victory zone to look like than this one.

This is the statement of any champion who has fought well and emerged victorious. There were challenges and players who got injured and teams that were stronger. There were plays that were changed unfairly, rules that may have been broken, fouls committed, and physical, mental, and spiritual limitations from time to time during the game. You may even have experienced a total lack of faith in your ability to win from one play to the next. But you pressed into your choice for victory, dug your cleats in deeper, and ran harder—until you crossed the finish line a victor.

There is no greater achievement than that of someone who has truly overcome the odds to win the game. You have to see your life as no different than that of any athlete. Some days, you don't want to suit up and play—and on others, you can't wait to get on the court or take the field. For athletes, winning is mostly mental. It takes tremendous discipline combined with great mental resolve to achieve a victory. Life is the same. You have to be mentally resolved in your choice for victory. If you are not, you will hinder yourself.

You need discipline in every war zone—and even more in your victory zone, lest you become entangled by the rewards. Victory, when you have overcome much, can become vain, selfish, and vapid if you aren't resolved to continue to fight the brokenness of your victimization and spiritual shortcomings, even while winning. Often, we see people who have pushed past many trials and tribulations to achieve victory only to get tripped up in a war zone that still contains unresolved conflict. This leaves many people who have become extremely successful miserable and unhappy when they should be celebrating a life fulfilled. It only proves that victory on the outside means nothing without victory on the inside.

Even in victory, the choice for victory is to be made daily.

Culture and the Victory Zone

For many today, victory looks like many things. For some, it looks like being able to provide an education for their children. For some, it looks like a promotion at work. For others, it looks like the end of poverty, abuse, and racial injustice.

For me, victory has taken on many profound and simple forms. I am a woman who, in spite of the injustices I've experienced, do not see myself defined by my abuses or by my abusers. I don't see myself as a victim. I see myself as able to do all things through Christ who strengthens me. I see myself as someone with choices and the power to choose victory over any obstacle. Mostly, I am a woman who finally chose a great husband and father.

If you read the victim's narrative my personal war zone prepared for me, marriage was not in the cards. If you understood the spiritual war zone in my life, you would see that a healthy son was not included in the narrative written for me. My victory zone includes a husband who adores me and a son who has grown up to be an incredible young man.

I wear victory well. It looks much younger and is more likable than the clothes worn by a victim. My victory zone is not sin-free because I am not perfect. I still fight in my spiritual war zone to grow and become more effective in my choice for victory. I am resolved to wage war daily to walk, talk, and think like God's daughter, worthy of the calling and purposes for my life.

The victory zone is an amazing one to get to because it means you've done the work! But victors know the battle is not over. We are in a constant push to elevate culture.

America is going through a culture shift. Victims of traumatic events, such as physical and sexual abuse, have begun to speak out en masse. It is good that many harmful acts that have been hidden for years are finally being investigated and even prosecuted. Shining light on darkness is always a good thing.

However, victim classification is now in vogue—so much so that many born-again believers live with a victim mentality rather than in the victory secured by Christ. So how do we experience Christian victory in a culture of victims?

There's no greater example of this than Jesus, the One who makes our victory possible. He certainly experienced unjust treatment. He was victimized. Yet He *never* embraced a victim's mentality. He never complained, wanted to quit, felt like someone owed Him something for His trials, or doubted that He could achieve victory. Imagine if He was too angry, fearful, or entitled to die on the cross—something He did for even those harming Him.

Clearly, there is a huge difference between the abuse Jesus endured and the physical abuse or injustice you may be experiencing today. Jesus gave Himself to the cross. He left Heaven for one purpose—to pay for the sins of all humanity. But I also call your attention to Hebrews 12:3: *"For consider Him who has endured such hostility by sinners against Himself, so that you will not grow weary and lose heart"* (NASB).

Although Jesus was completely innocent, He endured the most corrupt trial in human history. In a public spectacle, He was mocked, shamed, and beaten beyond recognition by those He would forgive. However, this was not the last chapter.

The cross is about payment for sin, but the resurrection is about the power to overcome. Jesus rose from the grave in victory—not vengeance. He rose as a victor, shedding the garments of victimization and leaving them in the grave. The choice you face is to rise or to remain. Rise in victory, or remain a victim. If you choose to rise, your choice requires your mind and heart to make a commitment to victory. Then the battle against your personal life circumstances, challenges, and injustices begins.

I won't ever forget the moment I surrendered to Christ. It was years after I was born again. I had accepted Christ, but I wasn't living as if I knew much about Him; there was still much to learn. I often say I was saved but not surrendered. That left me still in jeopardy of Hell. In the moment of surrender, something very different occurred. I died to sin in order to rise again to victory. My victory choice really happened then. There is this moment of knowing you are willing to die to all that you think, know, and are to become whatever God wants. It is a moment of death and life, a moment of rebirth. It was then that I identified with the power of His resurrection, which secured my victory over whatever this life brings.

"Who will separate us from the love of Christ? Will tribulation, or distress, or persecution, or famine, or nakedness, or peril, or sword? Just as it is written, "For your sake we are being put to death all day long. We were considered as sheep to be slaughtered." But in all these things we overwhelmingly conquer through Him who loved us" (Romans 8:35–37 NASB).

Your personal set of challenges and injustices requires you to commit to bringing every thought captive to Christ. That is how you'll create the mindset of a victor rather than a victim. I love how the evangelist Bucky Kennedy puts it: "I choose not to dwell in the pain of my past. Instead, I choose to walk in the promise and reality of who 'He is.' He is my Rock, my Refuge, my Defender, my Deliverer, my Shepherd, my Shield, and my Salvation." He'll be that for you, too, if you choose.

Having the mind of Christ also means that we must choose to forgive. I have spoken much about forgiveness because it's at the core of who we are as Christians.

Those who've imposed cruelty on you might not ever ask for your forgiveness. Sadly, my many offenders have yet to find the words, "I am sorry. Please forgive me." But I don't have to define my life by how they have hurt me and what they owe me. You don't have to define your life by how you have been hurt either. I don't want your forty acres and a mule when my Father is capable of giving me the planet. Don't give in to the mindset of victimization. Ask the Lord to help you forgive simply because He forgave first. You and I can experience victory in a culture of victims by forgiving those who have victimized us and moving on with our lives. The choice to forgive is rooted in your need to be forgiven and your desire to be set free from the chains of unforgiveness. These chains only serve to keep you bound to your victim's mentality. The choice, again, is yours.

Everybody who lives in the world today wants to be like everybody else who lives in the world today. It's sad. It's as if everyone has lost their uniqueness. The good news is that in the victory zone, everyone is unique and confident in who they are. Victors do not seek to be like anybody but who they were created to be. They find their identity in the hands of the One who created them. Your past is a weapon you will learn to wield for good in the victory zone of your life. It is not your nemesis; it's your strength.

In your victory zone, you will be tempted to give in to exhaustion because the journey may have been hard and the battles long. But if you cling to the hope that propelled you into your choice to be a victor no matter what, you will be given all the strength you need.

Choosing victory is more than choosing to be successful financially or in worldly terms. Choosing victory is about choosing life. It's about choosing to get up even though you may have been knocked down. It's about accepting responsibility for your part. Often, your part is only to do the right thing, take the higher road, and forgive.

Making life choices that align with God's will is victory. Victors understand that the battles have been the Lord's all along. They have peace that future ones will be equally attended to. No matter what victors face, they choose to find the victory in it.

Jesus was victorious over sin and the grave. Therefore, your choice is backed up by the power of the cross. We can live in the reality of *His victory* at work in *our lives*. In your decision to remain chained to old ways of thinking and living—or not—I ask you one final question:

How is defining yourself as a victim working out for you?

If the answer is, "It isn't," then the choice for victory is right in front of you. Life doesn't get easier because you make the choice to move from victim to victor. *Life just gets clearer that there is no other choice to make that leaves you moving forward.* We are not here to live backward. In fact, it's living backward, chained to our past, stuck in our history, that destroys people and nations.

Faith is putting one foot in front of the other when you desire to walk. Although we are capable of walking backward, we were created to walk forward. Victory is forward motion, often pulling yourself and others around you out of a grave. You were created to live in the victory zone, and victory is your battle cry in the various war zones you must confront. The victory zone is for you once you make the simple decision that no matter how much life has thrown at you or will throw at you, you will choose victory for yourself and your loved ones. Nobody else owes you the life you desire, but your choice to change your circumstances is something you owe yourself. Your children benefit. Your fellow citizens benefit. You benefit.

Culturally, the world wants you to be angry. It wants you to embrace your personal victim's narrative and build a life around it. However, you know down inside there is nowhere positive you can go with a mind diseased by narratives that include anger, lack, and hopelessness. These victim's narratives are exhausting.

But the victor's narrative includes success, happiness, and freedom of the mind. Victory in the culture we live in today may cost you your current despair, and possibly a friend or two, but it will also reward you with your desired life.

At the end of the day, all you have to do is *choose!*